JRD TATA AND THE ETHICS OF PHILANTHROPY

This book introduces readers to the ethics of philanthropy, particularly in the Indian context. Drawing on JRD Tata's philosophy and approach to business, it shows how business and philanthropy were intrinsically related for him. JRD Tata was arguably one of the most influential businessmen in post-Independence India. He was instrumental in not only expanding the Tata businesses but was also known for his impact on the conduct of business as well as his support for various national projects including research and education. He introduced key labour laws in his factories, which later became the model for the Indian government. He was also part of government institutions such as Air India.

By discussing ideas such as trusteeship, the notion of profit, the relation between public and private, and social welfare, the book offers an intellectual map of JRD's thoughts and an original perspective on their significance for an ethics of philanthropy in general. It provides new insights into the nature of ethical problems in the Indian context as well as ways to negotiate with them based on JRD's work and reflections. It further creates a more meaningful understanding of Corporate Social Responsibility in the present global economy.

Lucid and comprehensive, this book will be useful to scholars, researchers and faculty in departments of management and business studies, social work, sociology, economics and philosophy, as well as across social sciences. It will be of great interest to philanthropy organisations, non-governmental organisations, business schools, industry bodies, corporates, and those in leadership and management.

Sundar Sarukkai was Professor of Philosophy at the National Institute of Advanced Studies, Bengaluru, India, until 2019. He was also the Founder-Director of the Manipal Centre for Philosophy and Humanities, and has worked primarily in the philosophy of natural and social sciences. He has been part of studies on Gandhian and other social organisations as well as philanthropic ones. He is the author of *Translating the World: Science and Language* (2002), *Philosophy of Symmetry* (2004), *Indian Philosophy and Philosophy of Science* (2005), *What is Science?* (2012), and two books co-authored with Gopal Guru: *The Cracked Mirror: An Indian Debate on Experience and Theory* (2012/2017) and *Experience, Caste and the Everyday Social* (2019). He has also been active in outreach programmes to take philosophy to different communities and places, including philosophy workshops for children and bringing philosophy to the public through his writing in the media and through his initiative, Barefoot Philosophers.

JRD TATA AND THE ETHICS OF PHILANTHROPY

Sundar Sarukkai

Routledge
Taylor & Francis Group

LONDON AND NEW YORK

First published 2020
by Routledge
2 Park Square, Milton Park, Abingdon, Oxon OX14 4RN

and by Routledge
52 Vanderbilt Avenue, New York, NY 10017

Routledge is an imprint of the Taylor & Francis Group, an informa business

British Library Cataloguing-in-Publication Data
A catalogue record for this book is available from the British Library

Library of Congress Cataloging-in-Publication Data
A catalog record has been requested for this book

ISBN: 978-1-138-20379-2 (hbk)
ISBN: 978-0-367-48712-6 (pbk)
ISBN: 978-1-003-04240-2 (ebk)

Typeset in Bembo
by Taylor & Francis Books

CONTENTS

ACKNOWLEDGEMENTS

The book originally came into being in 2005 at the suggestion of Dr K. Kasturirangan, then Director of the National Institute of Advanced Studies (NIAS), Bangalore. The occasion was the centenary-year celebration of JRD Tata in 2004. NIAS was among the last major institutional initiatives undertaken by JRD, and to commemorate JRD's centenary, Dr Kasturirangan thought it would be fitting to produce a small volume on him. Without any hesitation, I agreed to Dr Kasturirangan's suggestion as I had for quite some time wanted to explore JRD's ideas since I felt that in his philosophy lay a possibility of finding newer paradigms for social development in today's world. For over a decade I had heard about JRD, mainly as a consequence of coordinating a course for senior executives from various government and private industries every year at NIAS. In every course, while informally talking to the participants, which included senior bureaucrats, I would be surprised at how much respect they all had for JRD, even those who belonged to business groups in competition with the Tatas.

But then the manuscript was put on the backburner for various reasons. I left NIAS in 2009 and it was upon my rejoining it in 2016 that the late Prof Baldev Raj, then Director of NIAS, who had read the manuscript, insisted that the book be published. But I wanted to add another chapter to the original manuscript in order to give a context for the book. Now, in 2019, I wanted to reposition this book in terms of what I had set out to do initially. Reflecting on my own interest in social change and philanthropy, the chapter I added was on the ethics of philanthropy. During the hiatus, I had the opportunity to study some Gandhian organisations and over the last two years was really fortunate to have had an opportunity to understand some of the issues more deeply because of a prolonged engagement with the Azim Premji Philanthropic Initiatives in Bangalore. I realised that one of the great challenges in this field is the lack of enough material about the ethical aspects of philanthropy, and hence this small attempt.

I am especially grateful to Dr Kasturirangan for having catalysed this work in the first place and to Dr Baldev Raj for having insisted on reviving it. This project was also greatly helped by Dr J. J. Irani who also made possible my visits to the JRD archives at Pune and also the Tata archives at Jamshedpur.

The staff at these archives were instrumental in helping me find appropriate material. Thanks to Mr Raghunath for going out of his way to facilitate my work in the Pune archive. My gratitude to Mr Narla who helped me with various computer files. Thanks also to Mr Raju for cheerfully doing all the hard work carrying files from one place to another! Similarly, the support at the Centre for Excellence in Jamshedpur must also be acknowledged. Ms Jenny Shah, in spite of her hectic schedule, managed to find time to help me with various visits. Mr Swarup in the archives was not only helpful but also patient with my various requests.

I was able to get detailed information on the social welfare schemes from Mr R. K. Singh in Jamshedpur. He not only spent his valuable time and energy in answering my incessant questions but also arranged for visits to some of their programmes, which gave me a good idea about the efficacy of these programmes. Many thanks to him! It is also a pleasure to thank Mr H. Jha who was kind enough to not only show me around a plant but also spent valuable time talking about JRD.

I am also grateful to Dr Jon Wilson for his interest in the book; his comments reignited my interest in this book. I am grateful to Rangan Varadan for all his inputs, to Samir Banerji who has always been my sounding board on Gandhi and to K. V. Akshara for discussions related to philanthropy in the arts. I learnt much from many people at the Azim Premji Philanthropic Initiatives (APPI), Bangalore and I want to most sincerely thank all of them for giving me an insight into the day-to-day work of philanthropy and for so openly and graciously sharing their thoughts and concerns on philanthropy.

As always, Dhanu was an indispensable part of the many discussions that are reflected in this book and I can't thank her enough. In particular, working with her on the report we produced for APPI was extremely important to my understanding of the issues surrounding philanthropy. The chapter on trusteeship was earlier published as part of a volume on *Zoroastrianism* by the Project of History of Indian Science, Philosophy and Culture (PHISPC), Centre for Studies in Civilizations, and I thank Dr Murzban Jal and PHISPC for publishing that article.

1

INTRODUCTION

There is more than one way of capturing the spirit of individuals who have had an impact on society. A common approach is to write a biography, which would trace their life story. Or one could write a philosophical biography, which would analyse their philosophy. This book has more affinity with the latter. The subject of analysis is Jehangir Ratanji Dadabhoy Tata, affectionately known as JRD, one of the most important influences in India in the last century. Historical biographies of JRD are already available; what is needed at this stage is an analysis of his ideas to complement those biographies. Such an analysis would address questions such as: What were the ideas that drove JRD? What notions were his actions based upon? What principles were fundamental to JRD, both in his personal and professional lives? What philosophical themes underlie his ethics? This book attempts to answer some of these and related questions.

Analysing a person's thoughts and understanding the reasons behind their actions is a challenging task, especially when the individual does not explicitly explain such reasons. It is a difficult task to attempt this even for an ordinary person and in the case of JRD it only gets that much more difficult. Not only was he one of the foremost industrialists in the country, he had also established a reputation for ethical conduct unparalleled in the business world. He was a leader not only of the Tata group of companies but also an acknowledged leader of the Indian private sector. He revolutionised labour welfare and introduced some of the most important innovations in corporate involvement in social welfare schemes. In between doing all this, he was supporting initiatives to set up world-class research institutes and hospitals. As if this were not enough, he started the first airline in India, Air-India. After its nationalisation, he agreed to be its Chairman, a position he held for more than two decades during which time he established it as one of the premier airlines in the world.

How then does one approach the task of analysing a man who has accomplished all this and more? Perhaps even before this question can be answered, we need to ask why it is essential to make such an effort now.

For a man of his stature, JRD's visibility in the public sphere was comparatively less than it ought to have been. For a man who was instrumental in setting ethical standards for big business and industry, one who exemplified service not just to the nation but also to the underprivileged, his words and actions have been most underplayed.

This is a matter of great surprise. Why is it that a man who had accomplished so much, who was not only a leader of business but also of philanthropy and ethical conduct, who actively and materially supported teaching and research along with social welfare, is so little analysed and talked about today? This neglect is all the more contradictory when we find that people from different walks of life hold JRD in great respect, as was well manifested in the people's reaction on his receiving the nation's highest award, the Bharat Ratna. JRD's abiding regret was that the government never drew on him enough to discuss what could be done to deal with many of India's economic and other problems.

However, there is a great need now to learn how to engage with his ideas effectively and to draw inspiration from them. It is more than two decades since the world has undergone the paradigmatic change of globalisation. Among other aspects, it has also brought about monumental changes in the nature of business, free market enterprise and, equally importantly, it has increased the public fascination with capitalism and consumerism. Now business organisations, in this transnational avatar, have become very powerful, some of them more powerful than some nations. The pace of change is extremely rapid, thereby leaving little time for reflection of the consequences of this change or even the mechanisms of change.

In such a scenario, who better to draw upon than JRD, for JRD first and foremost belonged to the community of these entrepreneurs. At the same time, he was also different from them in his expectation of business and its responsibility to the world and human society. Thus, if we are to meaningfully develop the human face of globalisation, JRD would be one of the important thinkers who would be relevant.

The strategy of reading and analysing JRD began by isolating some of the most important themes for him, themes to which he himself had accorded attention. I was particularly interested in those ideas related to philanthropy. In going through the material in his archives, I found to my surprise that his business practices were all intrinsically related to philanthropy in one way or the other. I believe that it is possible to argue that, for JRD, *business without philanthropy could not be imagined.* I then explored some of the basic presuppositions implicated in these themes, explorations which might give an insight into why those themes were so important to JRD. My exploration and extension of JRD's ideas was mediated by his succinct remarks about many of them. In exploring the foundations of JRD's ideas, I was basically attempting to expand the discourse that will become available to us in talking about JRD. Without such an expanded discourse, it would be difficult to engage with his worldview in the context of other ideas and other actions.

Then, in tune with JRD's spirit, I decided to expand and engage with those themes that were central to understanding JRD. In so doing, my own professional affiliation with philosophy might have influenced the presentation of this material. This is not undesirable, however, since I began this task by trying to understand JRD's philosophy of life and action, and to show how it is related to his views on philanthropy as an essential component of business.

It is for this reason that I begin with the chapter on the ethics of philanthropy (Chapter 2). This is a topic that is becoming extremely important today as philanthropic institutions are growing and are having an impact on the larger society. It is the case that most philanthropic organisations are run with money generated by business corporations. They use funds to make a difference to people in various ways: supporting government schools, funding nutrition programmes for the poor, funding shelters for the homeless and the destitute, and so on. In doing this, they are often doing the job of the government but are not accountable to the public as is the government. This leads to many interesting ethical dilemmas. This chapter lists some of these dilemmas and introduces the reader to the basic approach in the discipline of ethics in order to clarify the exact nature of the ethical issues in philanthropy. There are no easy answers to ethical dilemmas in philanthropy. What we can learn from JRD is that the ethics of philanthropy needs us to make modifications in our cherished beliefs about ideas such as profit, trusteeship, private, public and responsibility.

Chapter 3 deals with trusteeship, a theme which illustrates JRD's practical manifestation of responsibility. This is also one of the most important themes in human social thought and one which is at the core of philanthropy. JRD was inspired and influenced by Gandhi's idea of trusteeship where he argued that people who own wealth should deal with that wealth as if they are trustees of it. Being a trustee of one's wealth means that we only manage that wealth as a trustee for the benefit of the community, nation and those who are deprived. For Gandhi, the rich had to relate to their wealth as if they were managing that wealth for the welfare of others. Thus, the idea of trusteeship makes us re-examine what we mean by ownership of wealth. I believe that a useful way to analyse the notion of ownership is by looking at how we view our 'own' wealth. We can relate to our wealth in two different ways: with a sense of authority or with a sense of responsibility. The former way of looking at it would imply that we can do what we want with our wealth, since it is 'our' wealth anyway. However, if the meaning of one's 'own' wealth is only to have a sense of responsibility then we are accountable to how we administer and spend this wealth. This view brings to the fore again the notion of responsibility. Trusteeship brings responsibility to our doorsteps in the sense that we have to act with a sense of responsibility towards all our possessions as if they belonged to everybody else. Gandhi practised what he preached but he was more interested in making such a system socially practicable and viable. In trying to make this possible, Gandhi privileged the role of the State to make sure the wealth of rich, private citizens was placed under some trusteeship scheme.

JRD lived his life imbued with the spirit of trusteeship. He went on record many times over emphasising that he only saw himself as a trustee not only of his wealth but also of his time and capabilities. To him, the notion of a trustee would have best captured the essence of responsibility. He, like Gandhi, practised what he preached; he lived as a trustee and administered his wealth as a trustee. In the literal sense, all his wealth was given to Trusts and even in the last period of his life his personal wealth was miniscule compared to what would be expected for a person of his position. Like the other Tatas before him, who had also given away their wealth to Trusts which supported various programmes in the country, he too gave up his wealth for his Trust. From being a trustee of his wealth, he demanded that his companies also function as trustees. In making this demand, he was bringing corporates and business into the domain of trusteeship and in so doing he institutionalised the act of trusteeship, a move which I think was his most important contribution to this idea. JRD's experiments with trusteeship once again illustrate his emphasis on the pragmatic and practical, and not on the theoretical. However, as I mentioned earlier, there are many theoretical issues associated with trusteeship and with JRD's practical demonstration of it.

Chapter 4 discusses some of these issues by first analysing the relation between business and social welfare. In the context of social welfare and social work, there has been a strong, dominant tradition of voluntarism. However, can something as important as social change, particularly in the lives of the underprivileged, be left to a voluntary spirit? The history of social reform movements exhibit how some of these movements lose their momentum and vision once the individual who was the motivating leader is no longer a part of the movement. Also, when one individual dies or leaves the movement, how can we make sure that the movement continues its important work? Leaving it all to voluntarism has sometimes negated this continuity since the people who inherit these movements may not share the vision of the original activist. For JRD, it was important to continue this work and make it less dependent on a particular individual's vision. One way to do this was to professionalise social work; this is what JRD did in incorporating departments in the Tata companies which would deal professionally with various social welfare programmes. Making these programmes professional implies that the people who work in these programmes also become accountable. In the earlier model of voluntarism, accountability was often a casualty. This chapter discusses some of these issues in some detail and also notes the problems of professionalisation.

Social audit is the new mantra of corporates these days. JRD was the pioneer in this, like in many other fields, in India. TISCO was the first company, private or public, that voluntarily conducted a social audit in 1981. Ten years later, they had another social audit. This chapter also discusses some aspects of social audit and why it has become suddenly prominent in the vocabulary of the private sector. I also summarise the two social audit reports since they illustrate well what kinds of social programmes have been supported by Tata Steel. Through this we can see clear manifestations of their commitment to social welfare and of fulfilling their role as a trustee. The trusteeship idea inherent in JRD is also manifested in pioneering labour welfare schemes in the Tata companies. Many of these labour schemes were made into government laws long after their implementation in the Tata companies. JRD's approach to labour was also in the spirit of trusteeship as was also his commitment to the town of Jamshedpur.

Finally, this chapter ends with a discussion on the theme of 'balance' that, in my view, most influenced JRD's practical approach to life and business. Although JRD himself did not write much about the principle of balance, what little he did clearly exemplified its importance. As I argue, it is clear that the notion of balance lies at the foundation of JRD's philosophy since he was forever trying to balance various contrary factors and influences. In most of his formulations, we find him attempting to strike a 'fine' balance – whether it was between duty and responsibility, autonomy and accountability, private and public, profit and service, professionalism and voluntarism, power and control, freedom and sacrifice, and so forth. I believe that a philosophy of balance best represents JRD's philosophy, and best explains his attitudes and actions. In principle, a philosophy of balance is very desirable as it does not give in to extreme positions, always attempts to mediate between contrary and contradictory pressures, is much more sensitive to a plural society and so on. JRD's personal life also shows his constant attempt to reach a balance in all that he did.

The next two chapters use JRD's ideas to critically reflect on some concepts that are essential to philanthropy and its relation to business. In Chapter 5, I analyse the notions of private and public that are necessary to understand JRD's important insight, one which he voiced repeatedly, that turned some of these meanings upside down. JRD insisted that the private should exhibit responsibility and the public should have more autonomy. His clearest articulation of this is in the context of the private and public sectors, but this theme of bringing together freedom (autonomy, private) and responsibility, and similarly, responsibility (accountability, public) and autonomy is necessary for understanding many of his views on social welfare and his emphasis on social responsibility. I begin by discussing different ways of understanding the notions of the private and the public, followed by an analysis of the ideas of autonomy and accountability. There is yet another theme which can be usefully explored, which is that of power and control. The ideas of power and control are not only important in a social context but also in individual relationships. They are also philosophically interesting topics in the sense that they are characteristics which are an essential part of human nature. JRD confronted the problem of power and control throughout his professional life. What brings these ideas together is his emphasis on responsibility, one that is necessary not only in personal life but also in public space. For JRD, it was important that responsibility was not imposed from any authority but should be autonomous. Thus, we can see how freedom and duty are essentially bound together and for him duty was also a freedom, a choice one makes consciously. JRD extended this notion of responsibility from the individual to companies and thereby initiated the notion of social responsibility for corporates.

An important theme is that of profit, which is discussed in a broader sense in Chapter 6. If there is one idea that is essentially related to that of business, it is the idea of profit. Profit distinguishes business from other activities. But what exactly is profit? How do we understand the nature of profit? The discipline of economics has, as to be expected, analysed this idea in great detail. However, I begin with exploring some simple ideas that are usually associated with profit. JRD had an expanded notion of profit and it is this expanded notion that served him in his own understanding of the nature of business. How is it possible to expand the meaning of profit in order to incorporate many of the terms that are usually kept outside its ambit? I look at two images that influence our understanding of profit: the zero-sum principle and the organic growth model. Profit seen in a quantitative sense or only with respect to the individual/private cannot be the sense of profit that concerned JRD. The very meaning of profit has to be expanded to include not only profit in a qualitative sense but also to incorporate profit across time and space, thereby not restricting profit to the localised perspective of the individual or the private. For JRD, two other related concepts were very important. These were the means towards profit and the uses of profit. Both means and uses are circumscribed by various responsibilities and duties. In this sense, the ownership of profit is a profound issue and I believe that we can understand JRD's insight into this theme by critically analysing the question: To whom does profit belong?

In exploring the theme of profit, we come across various other themes that demand explanation and explication. First of all, the theme of private and public is extremely important not only for JRD but also for business and, in fact, for society. What constitutes the private and the public? How did these categories come about? Are they naturally given? The original model of the private is the individual, that which resides in our own personhood. And the first site of the public is the community around the individual. Why are the notions of private and public placed in opposition to each other? For JRD, the question of private and public is at the core of his views on business because the private–public distinction is also manifested in the business sector. In today's world, it is no longer easy to distinguish the public from the private since the representatives of the public are dominantly private entrepreneurs and the private has moved into matters related to the public through their growing influence with the government and through philanthropy.

For a long time, businesses have been categorised as belonging either to the private or the public sector, especially in the case of industries. Along with this distinction, there are various other consequences such as the association of autonomy with the private and accountability with the public. The idea of the private privileges individual human autonomy. This autonomy is responsible for many of the cherished beliefs of capitalism and private business in general. When the human individual becomes sacrosanct and becomes the centre of the universe as it were, then notions such as privacy, secrecy, individuality, creativity, autonomy and incentive become very important. Many of these notions get carried over into the meaning of the 'private' sector. Similarly, public entities are defined by various meanings such as openness, accountability, responsibility, and the interests of the group prevailing over those of the individual.

Some may want to make a distinction between the ethics of a person and his or her public action but, as Gandhi and JRD show, such distinctions cannot be tenable. JRD's ethics of business and philanthropy is also reflected in his personal life and this is discussed in Chapter 7. An individual cannot be described in terms of many stories and anecdotes alone. To construct the individual it is important to explore and analyse not just the positions they held, their actions and their desires but also their personal proclivities. While the earlier chapters tried to flesh out themes that will help us understand JRD as the thinker and doer, this chapter tries to explore JRD as a human being. But this is a task that is not only beyond the limitations of a chapter but is also one that needs a separate book! Moreover there are biographies which give us a good portrait of him. I intrude into his personal space only in the context of making sense of his personal makeup which influenced many of the themes discussed earlier in the book. Thus, I focus exclusively on one aspect of his personality that, at least to me, explains best his actions, and this is the idea of human empathy. JRD was one who enjoyed living and exhibited a spirit that mixed the adventurous and the mundane effortlessly. This spirit was also a celebration of individuality. JRD's individuality was based not on defining it in contrast to others but in contrast to his own abilities. Thus, he constructed himself in terms of his own limitations and boundaries and not in terms of other people's limitations. It is not an accident that competitive sports were not as important to him as individual sporting activity.

This act of defining himself not in opposition to others but only through the strengths and limitations of his own capabilities is one that is also manifested in his business practice. In contemporary times, the importance of competition and winning against others has become the defining character of the age. The strength of an individual is defined in terms of the success the individual has against others and not on any intrinsic ability. JRD did not accept such a principle either in the conduct of his life or his business.

The chapter concludes with a discussion on the importance of personal ethics to social ethics. JRD's well-known ethical practices in business cannot be separated from his personal ethics. Rather than describe and list his personal ethical outlook, I focus on one significant illustrative example, that of his letter writing. JRD wrote and replied to thousands of letters, some from people he knew but most from people he didn't. I discuss a few examples of his replies to some letters which illustrate an empathy, a characteristic that is found in many other facets of his personal and public life. I then conclude with a few remarks on the challenges to JRD's vision for the group which he led for so many decades with great dignity.

This book does not explore or analyse his business capabilities in terms of economics or management techniques. It is primarily concerned with his philosophical outlook and, in particular, with the relation between business and philanthropy. It is an attempt to show how JRD's approach to business was intrinsically sensitive to the ethical questions concerning philanthropy and how, for him, business could not in principle be decoupled from the philanthropic imagination. This book is an attempt not to send JRD into a museum where his ideas could be revered from a distance but rather to make him a living presence among us by debating, engaging, critiquing and extending his ideas.

2

ETHICS OF PHILANTHROPY

It is often said that the idea of philanthropy is a comparatively new idea that arose in a particular context in the US. Although somewhat similar to earlier practices associated with charity and individual acts of giving prevalent in many traditions, philanthropy was defined as a different enterprise. So when it is said that India had no tradition of philanthropy, it must be seen as a comment more on the professionalisation of giving rather than on the broader culture of giving itself. But if philanthropy is seen as a professional act of distributing wealth from the rich to not just the needy individuals but also to a 'needy' government and society, then it is indeed useful to make a distinction between philanthropy and charity. Charity can take various forms ranging from giving money to beggars, donating to religious organisations, or giving funds for education, medical or other needs to individuals on a voluntary basis. But philanthropy is an institutionalisation of these acts and more. Primarily because of this institutionalisation, as well as the effect of philanthropy on communities and groups rather than isolated individuals alone, the question of ethics becomes absolutely essential to the task of philanthropy. The question of ethics arises automatically when our actions impact other humans and other systems, such as the environment, which can affect other humans. Thus, both individual and institutional actions should be governed by principles of right and wrong action, and by moral principles and ethical codes. These ideas are more important in the Indian context since the line between philanthropy and social engineering is becoming very thin due to the social power of the philanthropists as well as the vision that drives their philanthropy.

In this chapter, I will highlight some basic ethical questions that arise in philanthropy, with particular reference to India. In the chapters that follow, I will illustrate how JRD Tata's approach to his life and business could be seen as ways of establishing the underlying principles of philanthropy that were an essential component of his worldview.

Philanthropic organisations typically work in areas such as health, education, nutrition, poverty alleviation, supporting vulnerable groups and giving scholarships. The focus of philanthropy is a broad canvas that includes the nation as well as communities within it. Thus, the scope of philanthropic action includes the following: doing good for the nation (a form of service to the nation), taking leadership within a society/community, enabling excellence in arts, academics and other valued activities in a society, and, for some, enabling ethical values with respect to treatment of humans and/or the environment. All such actions raise important ethical questions. Given the professionalisation of philanthropy, there are more such ethical issues in philanthropy as compared to the act of an individual giving money as charity. We will see in what follows that the Tatas have always envisioned philanthropy along these broader lines such as service to the nation and creating excellence in many domains. I will first begin with a discussion on ethical dilemmas that are specific to philanthropy and then briefly introduce some salient points of ethics as a discipline.

Specific ethical dilemmas arising in philanthropy

Philanthropic institutions are well established in India and abroad, and they have already disbursed a significant amount of money to society. What kind of ethical issues arise in this process? Just because they give money 'away for free', does it mean that they are not answerable for their actions? If they are answerable, then to whom? What type of responsibilities and answerability can we expect from those who want to do 'good' to others?

The ethics of philanthropy is a new field of study.[1] However, much of the discussion seems to be focused on models of giving, whom to give to and how much to give. Should one give to change systems or individuals? Should one give so as to maximise the benefit of giving a particular amount of money? These and other similar questions become important when funds are distributed over time and in a consistent manner. In general, there are dilemmas that are common to any philanthropic activity across the world. Since some of the major philanthropic organisations such as the Tata Trusts, Azim Premji Philanthropic Initiatives, Bill and Melinda Gates Foundation and others have strong ties to business, I will focus on a subset of the relation between business and philanthropy. Some of the challenges that arise in this case are also applicable to the broader practice of philanthropy by individuals and others. The reason I restrict myself to the cases mentioned above is primarily because I want to understand JRD Tata through the prism of philanthropy and examine how his approach to business influenced his approach to giving and, at the same time, how his emphasis on giving influenced his approach to business. There is much that we can learn from this dynamic relation embodied in JRD Tata.

The issues that I highlight below are those that have arisen from engaging with the experiences of both funders and fundees (usually referred to as 'beneficiaries' in funding parlance) in India.

- **Inherent asymmetry:** The major problem in philanthropy is the inherent asymmetry between the giver and the receiver, between the funder and the fundee. This relation is always asymmetrical since one has money to give which the other needs. What are the ethical issues arising due to this asymmetry? Will this lead to power asymmetry? Does the funder have 'power' over the fundee? For example, there are NGOs who have been working in the field for decades. But when the funder gives money to this NGO, they intervene in various ways: by choosing what component to support, by making the NGOs conform to various financial and administrative rules that are applicable to business concerns and corporates, by pushing and nudging the NGOs to change their practices. A common clash that we have often observed is that between the field experience of the NGOs and the funders' worldview, which is not informed by the nature of the field in the same way as the NGO.

- **Perceived motivations for philanthropy:** Why does a person or a group want to give their money away? How do the receivers understand this giving? Is this giving a transaction, a kind of contract? Or is it a giving without any strings attached to it? Some receivers of funds feel that they are not obligated to the funders in any sense. Some of them have even taken the position that the funders are doing it for some reason of their own. These reasons may range from ideological beliefs about how people should live their life to the conviction that philanthropy is a form of social engineering that can (and should) be the goal of philanthropy.

- **Benefits to the funder:** Can the funder expect anything at all from the fundee? Can they 'demand' something for the support they give? Can accountability be asked for the money given to somebody as philanthropy? If there are expectations, then does philanthropy become a form of lending?

- **Origin of the money:** Does it matter who is giving the money? Or how the money is generated in the first instance? These questions are actually related to a broader concern about businesses and the project of generating profits. Is a company setting aside some of its profits to distribute as philanthropy? Can a business concern take a decision on this by itself? Is it a problem to take money from a business that does not have good business practices or a good public image?

- **Accountability:** What kind of projects and communities should be supported? If philanthropy intervenes in those areas which the government is supposed to be taking care of, such as health, water or education, then is the organisation ending up doing the government's work? The main reason that this issue becomes such a critical ethical problem is that when the government intervenes in society there are many measures of accountability. The officials, including politicians, who are supposed to enable certain interventions can be questioned and held accountable in principle. But in philanthropy, can there be any accountability? Should there be accountability? Or should we just say that since money is being given due to the 'goodwill' of the funder, we should not expect any serious measures of accountability from either side?

- **Domain knowledge:** How should one support the poor and the dispossessed? How much knowledge should the funders have of the situation before they intervene? Sometimes trying to help without proper understanding of the field may be more disastrous than not helping at all.
- **Scope of support:** Typically, philanthropic interventions are within a small segment of the population. (The government, on the other hand, is responsible for the whole population. This is another important distinction between them.) Is it correct to support a small segment of the community while the problems continue in other parts of the community? How many financial strictures should be put on NGOs? Is it right to fund for a few years and then get out? (Ratan Tata in an interview on philanthropy points to the effects of stopping funding and adds how they became 'most hated' when they stopped funding an initiative after some time.)[2] What are the effects of the intervention of the funder on the community? After the funder leaves, should they worry about how the community will be able to sustain itself without the support from the funder? Should they be political or non-political? Is it possible to be non-political? (For example, politicians can expect to get votes but can true philanthropy also be based on some expectations?)
- **Range of funding:** This is related to giving money not to the poor and the vulnerable but to artists and others who do work that is 'valued' by the funders. What vision will enable giving money to the arts? Can the 'values' and 'worldview' of the funder be imposed on the fundees?

These questions are largely ethical ones, by which I mean questions that deal with ethical concepts. They are not about the efficiency of distributing funds or even about their efficient usage. We can identify a set of concepts that are closely related to these ethical questions in these contexts. Many of these are commonly discussed in the literature.[3]

1. **Tainted money:** An important hurdle for fundees to negotiate is whether it is acceptable to use money derived from dubious means for philanthropy. To illustrate this problem, let me consider one extreme case. If a drug dealer who makes money illegally wants to give some of that money to philanthropy, would that be morally acceptable? Should the nature of business matter to their philanthropic work? There is an interesting parallel with Gandhi's argument that money made from the sales of alcohol should not be used to support schools. Such an issue is not a problem for private philanthropy per se since Gandhi was actually criticising the government's use of money which is obtained as tax from the sale of alcohol to fund its schools. But one can extend this argument of dubious origins to private businesses too. For instance, Gandhi considered that all profit arises from exploitation of one kind or another, and indeed there are many who speak about the making of profits through what is referred to in economics as the 'externalisation of costs'. All these involve ethical questions.

2. **Privacy and data:** When a funder funds an organisation, what can they expect in return? Can they get personal data from the beneficiaries? If so, what kind of use can they put this data to? For example, can the photos of people (including children) who are funded be used without explicit informed consent from the subjects? Can details about their lifestyle be shared with others? Or equivalently, do the funders have any 'rights' over data or even narratives of those who receive these funds?

3. **Self-regulation:** The deeper ethical question here arises from the fact that organisations and individuals who are given funds to continue their social work with communities may sometimes be so grateful for receiving money that they sign off on some things that they probably should not. So this means that the responsibility of regulation falls on the funders themselves. How then does one regulate oneself even while being in a position of 'helping' somebody else? Funders often do so by focusing on process-based disbursals which gloss over, or even conceal, ethical issues which arise in engaging with the social sector.

4. **Honesty and full disclosure:** Should the funders (and perhaps the business concern that they are associated with) share their intentions, motivations and long-term plans and vision with the communities they intervene in?

5. **Conflicts of interest:** Is there an ethical issue when a company helps a community in order to get an edge for their business? Often businesses have entered communities by supporting their cultural activities. Witness the business delegations that accompany foreign cultural organisations based in India.

6. **Unintended consequences:** While a philanthropist engages with a community to do some 'good', the end consequence might not turn out that way. So what should the ethical stance of philanthropy be in such situations? Are they responsible in any way? Do they just walk away after their funding ends? What kinds of responsibility and accountability does a philanthropist have?

7. **Partnership:** Equivalently, should the funders be true partners with the groups they work with? What does true partnership mean or imply? After all, the organisations on the ground have been working in the field for years, and the funders are only giving money – so what should the ethics of this relationship be? One specific issue in partnership is the following. Should the funders expect that the fundee organisation follow codes of conduct similar to their own? For example, let us say that there is an NGO which does not have the rules of hiring, gender practice and other norms that a funder might have. Just like the expectation of having uniformity of financial systems, should the funder expect that the NGO also follow their best practices with respect to employees etc.?

To get an idea of the kinds of approaches one could take to understand and address some of these dilemmas, I will give a brief outline of the kinds of ethical arguments one can make. Rather than look at these approaches as ones that will give unambiguous answers to how we should act, they should be understood as illustrating the strengths and weaknesses of the ethical positions we might take. Many of these dilemmas are also intrinsically related to the idea of profit and the role that profit plays in the functioning of a business enterprise. After setting out the basic questions that arise in the use of profits for the betterment of the social sector, I will then discuss various approaches in ethics.

The ethics of profit

Almost all of the biggest philanthropic organisations are related to business concerns. The money that these organisations use for their philanthropy is often taken from their business earnings. This is indeed a momentous and significant step since it is a moral act of a particular kind. It is an act that aims to redistribute wealth in more meaningful ways instead of just giving it away as charity. It also involves a lot of work and philanthropic organisations, in general, are themselves independent, professionally functioning entities. Although Business Ethics is comparatively a new field – some scholars place the origin in Raymond Baumhart's work in the 1960s – it has become prominent due to various public scandals that were global and of enormous magnitude, such as those in banking and trading. Today, business ethics is flourishing to a greater extent than the strictly philosophical study of ethics and has also become a mandatory course in degrees related to modern business and technology. The corporation as a business entity is a central concern in business ethics. In particular, the agency of the corporation, the modes of action of the corporation etc., are core issues in this field. Of growing interest is international business ethics, dealing with questions such as sensitivity to local cultures where business is conducted, negotiating with laws and customs which may be very different from those of the host country of the business concern, and so on. When these businesses also start a philanthropic arm, either through Corporate Social Responsibility (CSR) or independent of it, some of these ethical issues related to business ethics also become important in the ethics of philanthropy of these institutions.

Ethics matters to business in an essential sense. This is because of the intrinsic nature of business, which deals with profound and socially powerful ideas such as wealth, the creation of wealth, its distribution, the control of human labour, and creating a distinction between the public and the private. The ethically meaningful themes related to these acts include those of disparity, exploitation, the priority of profit over human rights and dignity, and the morally fluid category of greed.

If there is any one factor that has contributed to the growth of business ethics as a discipline, and indeed the public critique of business concerns, it is the growing inequality of wealth distribution in the world today. More than ever before in the history of human civilisation, fewer number of individuals own a disproportionate amount of the wealth of the world. By some accounts, a mere 5% of the world's population own nearly 70% of the wealth of the world. At the same time, there is growing poverty, and an increasing number of people are denied the basic comforts of housing, health and even food. With all this wealth in the world, there is still an extremely large number of people who die of hunger every year. This inequality is not the only problem facing businesses today. Many business concerns are valued very highly and some of them have budgets that are more than that of small nations. There is a constant proliferation of new products, new services, new sectors, and all of them can survive only by making a profit. The pressure on publicly owned companies to keep increasing their quarterly profits might eventually lead to a situation of collapse. Labour laws which protected the interests of workers are undergoing massive changes, particularly in the new business sector of IT. Business itself seems to be based on premises that are often ethically troubling: profits over human concerns, survival of the business at all costs, violation of labour laws, loss of work–life balance due to undue emphasis on pushing the bottom line, lack of effective regulation etc. There is definitely a sense of crisis facing contemporary society: the crisis of not knowing what to do about free-market business in a world which is already immersed in a neoliberal paradigm.

The fundamental ethical issue in business arises from the nature of business itself. If business is seen as a transaction that involves some notion of profit, then the ethical question is about the nature, utilisation and ownership of that profit. Has the profit been made in the 'right' way? If there is profit through unfair or illegal means then should the profit be seen as unethical? As mentioned before, for Gandhi, any organisation generating profit was doing so by engaging in 'exploitation'. Obviously, not all business transactions generate an ethical problem. For example, if a person buys a commodity for a certain price, adds her labour to it, and sells it at a higher price, there is a profit but that profit can also be seen as the cost of labour in facilitating that exchange. The question of ethics arises around the excess in this transaction. In India it is common to see this phenomenon: there are middlemen who buy tomatoes at a very cheap price and sell it at a much higher price. The farmers who grow the tomatoes get much less than what they deserve since the price at which people buy is far more than what the farmers get. So is there an ethical issue around the practice of middlemen? The middlemen might counter by saying that they facilitate the sale of the tomatoes and without them the farmers would not even be able to sell their commodity. Profit may thus be seen as the price paid to the middlemen for having taken a risk. But when there is a notion of excess or of exploitation, then ethical questions come to the surface.

Almost every business transaction in the broader commercial sphere will generate problems such as this. In modern terminology, the value added to a commodity can be much more than the cost of production. People pay money to acquire a commodity not only because of the commodity but because of the brand it is associated with. For example, a purse when branded by a well-known name becomes much more expensive than if the same purse is sold under another name. These value additions in between production and consumption are seen as a natural part of business practices today and so are not seen as having anything to do with ethics.

While there are many other ethical questions that arise in the way a business organisation works (including matters related to labour, human relations, transparency etc.), here I have tried to only highlight a fundamental tension between ethical action and profit making, which many would see as the essence of any business. This has an essential relation to philanthropy since most of the dominant philanthropic organisations have obtained their funds from business, as mentioned before. It is really the possibility of profit in the business sector that drives a large part of philanthropy today. However, the way some businesses have evolved is also an illustration of how a business can envision itself as doing something much more than merely making profit. And in doing so, it is already in the mode of philanthropy. For such businesses, philanthropy is integral to business decisions rather than philanthropy being an afterthought. In this book, I will argue that JRD Tata's approach to business exemplifies this internal relationship between philanthropy and business in all the businesses in which he was involved.

Ethics

Ethics is the analysis, as well as the development, of codes, of right and wrong action. It is a means of evaluating such actions, discovering the grounds on which we can make judgements of right and wrong, and helping in deciding how to act in a given situation. Many of us consider qualities such as kindness, humility, honesty, being respectful to others, empathy etc. as something to do with 'right' behaviour. We also consider certain actions, such as killing others, to be morally wrong. In more complex cases, some might consider paying bribes – and corruption in general – to be morally wrong. How do we come to these conclusions? Are we just following codes and rules given to us as children? Or are we expected to follow some reasoning to justify these actions?

The discipline of ethics is vast and complex. There are many assumptions we make when we invoke the idea of morality, and ethics as a discipline explores these presuppositions and foundations. For example, do we have special qualities such as moral qualities? Are these special only to humans or do other animals also have such qualities? If there are such qualities, what is their nature? Is it the same for all of us humans – for example, is kindness a virtue that all of us have 'naturally'? If so, how do we have it? Where is it to be found? Most importantly, why is it that we ourselves do not consistently act according to these qualities: a kind person is not always kind. Do these qualities differ in each one of us or are they similar? Often ethical qualities are related to emotional experiences, so is there a relation between ethics and emotions? Some philosophers argue that reason is the foundation for ethics and if so, is there a conflict between reason and emotion while making ethical decisions?

Another set of questions is about agency in ethical action. Is it the individual self who has to be ethical? Do we have agency when we act ethically? Is that decided by us – that is, is ethical action an autonomous decision by individuals? If so, do we reason and then act or do we just spontaneously act ethically? What is the nature of ethical action as against other actions like running, cooking etc.? Is ethical action different in kind from other kinds of actions?

A third set of questions is about social ethics. How does one function ethically in a society? How can we be ethical towards institutions and towards the larger society? For example, can individuals who are comparatively well off be indifferent to poverty within their society? If it is unethical to have such disparity of income, whose ethical problem is it – the individuals who belong to that society or the instruments of the society like the government? We can raise similar ethical questions about knowledge: is it even ethical to keep producing knowledge without worrying about the consequences? Similarly for desire. Is it unethical to keep desiring something? Is there something unethical about excessive spending on luxurious items? After all, remember it was Gandhi who said there is enough in this world for people's needs but not enough for their greed, thus making consumption itself an ethical issue. There are innumerable ethical issues that arise in the context of medical practice and with business practices.

Normally, the broader domain of ethics is broken down into three major subdivisions: *metaethics*, which deals with issues related to the principles and nature of ethics, *normative ethics*, which describes rules that govern ethical action, and *applied ethics*, which deals with a variety of subjects in which ethical questions are applied such as in medical ethics and business ethics.

As I pointed out earlier, a central ethical concern in business is related to profit. It is not possible to answer specific ethical questions about profit without drawing upon the psychology of humans, the nature of society, the duty one has towards the society, and so on. Given that there are many different theories of moral nature, there is appreciable complexity in formulating ethical responses even to simple ethical questions. Normative ethics deals with the analysis of normative claims on ethical action. For example, duty is a term which is commonly used when trying to decide between right and wrong action. People commonly use examples of not cheating others, taking care of family, not killing others as examples of duty. But why are these designated to be 'duties' and why are we obligated to follow them? Moreover, we normally follow duties only in some contexts but not in others. Killing is a good example. The belief that it is morally wrong to kill another human being is often violated in different contexts – for instance, killing in war, in self-defence, in capital punishment. The increased use of the language of rights is also a reflection of the emphasis on the value of duty, since rights and duties go together. Evaluating ethical action based on duties is very much a part of the ethical debates on business, ranging from claims that it is a duty to maximise one's potential to the belief that it is a moral duty to share one's wealth with those not as fortunate as oneself.

Another influential kind of normative ethics is consequentialist ethics, which is primarily the argument that we can evaluate the ethical status of an action by evaluating the consequences of that action. According to this view, there is nothing intrinsically right or wrong about any action but only in its consequences. Utilitarianism, ethical egoism, rational choice theory and other such approaches to resolving ethical issues fall under consequentialist ethics. These are also much used in arguments relating to business and corporate ethics.

Moving from the individual, we can consider similar questions in the case of institutions, groups, societies, nations and other such collectives. Just like human action can be right or wrong, so too can the actions of a collective like a community or a nation. But evaluating which actions are right or wrong is as complex in group actions as it is in individual action. If a nation goes to war and thereby causes the death of thousands of human beings, one cannot immediately say that this action is unethical since it may have been forced to go to a war to save its own people. However, some might hold the view that war is in itself unethical, independent of other arguments. Reservation in the Indian context can also be seen as an ethical response to the unethical practice of exclusion of certain communities from the benefits of values like education. A more common problem concerns the economic disparity within every society. For example, if a society has many rich people but also has a significant number of its people in extreme poverty, then there seems to be an ethical problem regarding whether such a situation can be allowed to continue. In such a scenario, ideas of redistributive justice could arise.

Core ethical principles and approaches

Ethical judgements are particular kinds of judgements. Often, it is not clear what kind of dilemmas are really ethical ones. Is corruption an ethical problem or an economic issue or a cultural attitude? Is it possible to clearly demarcate any problem into independent domains like this? One of the simple markers of an ethical issue is the use of principles and concepts that are largely ethical in nature. The moment concepts such as respect and dignity are used, then we may already be in the domain of the ethical.

Here, I will briefly give an outline of some of these principles and concepts, more as a simplified map of ethics. Whenever we encounter these principles and the concepts in them, we know we are in the space of ethics. Ethics has traditionally been about human beings, although it is now extended to ethical treatment of animals, ethical relationship with nature and so forth. In the context of humans, the question of ethics is largely about 'right' action towards other humans. In this, certain principles are largely taken as the foundation. For example, consider the concept of 'beneficence', which is about doing good for others. But as we are all aware, it is not always clear what is good for others. Who decides what is good for them? Even if those who receive support themselves decide, could they always be right? Hence the principle of 'non-maleficence' or not doing harm may become even more important in philanthropy as misguided charity can be quite damaging to communities. Similarly, imposing power (as in patriarchy) through the argument 'I am doing it only for your good' is also dangerous as it presumes an ignorance on the part of the beneficiaries about what is good for themselves, and it also compromises their autonomy to make decisions about their own life. Ethical theories try to define the various ways by which we can understand this notion of doing good for others. One popular idea in this context is the notion of 'greatest amount of good for greatest number of people'.

The notion of non–maleficence also leads to similar questions as in the case of beneficence. This is captured by the 'folk' moral lesson that if you cannot do good for others, at least do not harm them. Here again, the meaning of harming has to be carefully analysed. Not causing harm can have both positive and negative actions such as not causing harm/pain to humans, as well as not helping, being indifferent to, or manipulating others. Today we also include causing mental agony as a category of causing harm to others but deciding what is mental agony is still debatable.

One of the common approaches to this problem of doing good to others is the principle of 'Least Harm', which is basically the view that 'if all choices are bad, then the ethical choice is one with least harm'. Least harm includes not just the 'quantity' of harm done to a person but also the principle of 'harm to the fewest'.

Additional principles such as liberty, dignity and respect for all are now fundamental principles. We can use these principles as grounds for recognising what is right and what is wrong. For example, slavery is wrong on many of these counts including the denial of liberty, dignity and respect to those who are kept as slaves. A few more core ethical principles are those of equality (unbiased treatment of all people independent of gender, class, religion, caste and other social factors), autonomy of individuals (giving the right to individuals to make their choices and decisions) and the notion of trust that is necessary for most social actions. None of these terms is easily applicable. The complexity of understanding their meaning as well as their applicability in different contexts is what makes the discipline of ethics interesting as well as complex. For example, autonomy as a principle cannot immediately help resolve ethical issues. In the debate on abortion, the issues of autonomy have been quite complex: is the foetus under the mother's autonomy or can it have an independent autonomy? Does a woman, as an individual, have autonomy over her body? Does this autonomy imply that she can do what she wants to her body, especially if the foetus is seen as a part of her body? Can the State or her community have a right to what she should do with her body, including controlling how she should dress? In the case of medical ethics, the autonomy of patients is extremely important since doctors cannot do anything they want with the patient under the belief that they know more than the patient. Consent forms, as well as explanation of medical treatment, have become the official norm in hospitals today due to these ethical considerations. Medical research is another arena where rights of subjects have to be safeguarded during clinical trials so that ethical boundaries vis-à-vis human subjects are maintained even in the pursuit of knowledge.

Similarly, the notion of trust between humans translates into questions of confidentiality in various cases. In business, the problems related to insider trading, getting unfair benefit or using information for personal gain are directly related to trust as a central ethical norm. Confidentiality agreements, including an employee's record or complaints of sexual exploitation, are essential for any organisation to function in an ethical manner.

Relevant ethical theories

I have pointed out some of the key conceptual terms that signal the presence of an ethical issue. Their elaboration and analysis constitute ethical theories. There are many different theoretical approaches in ethics and I will highlight a few here, particularly those that are immediately relevant for philanthropy.

The branch of 'normative ethics' is about how one ought to act. The key term here is 'ought' – well exemplified by rules and commandments about our behaviour. But the meaning of 'ought' is not that simple. If somebody asks what one ought to do in a given situation, she is asking for something more than directions for action. What is often asked is the reason for why one ought to behave in a particular manner. Ethical theories try to perform this task of analysing the different possible meanings of terms like 'ought' in order to understand why some 'oughts' are important and some other rules are not really 'oughts'. For example, one could say that we ought to have qualities of kindness, empathy and charity. Or that we ought to treat all humans with dignity and respect. But why? What is this 'ought' based upon? One can either take these as foundational values of a community or one can make arguments for why it is preferable to have these qualities. We might say that being kind and empathetic will make our social life more harmonious and that treating others with dignity and respect will also make them treat us the same. However, if these are duties, we are then duty-bound to follow these qualities without worrying whether the consequence is good or not, or whether we get any benefit from acting in such a manner.

In the case of charity and philanthropy, there are similar questions. Should those who are better off take care of those who are not well off? Should philanthropy be seen as a duty for all business concerns that make a healthy profit? Should all of us have an attitude towards sharing our wealth with those not so fortunate? Is this a matter of something we ought to do? Similarly, we could say that treating others with dignity and respect is a duty and is not based on whether it will have a good consequence on our social life. Gandhi is a good example of a person for whom duty was often the most important quality of ethical action.

There are different approaches to these questions. One is based on the notion of virtue, another on duty. Two other theories evaluate ethical action through the evaluation of consequences of that action (consequentialist theories) and within that falls perhaps the most commonly invoked utilitarian theories.

Virtue theories argue that morality is not about particular moral rules that we are expected to follow but about acquiring good virtues such as honesty, courage, sincerity etc. If one has developed good virtues then presumably an act that we do based on these virtues will always be an ethical act. Thus, an act is to be evaluated by the goodness of the person/institution doing it and not the specificities of each action. So an action is judged by virtues and not by some specific actions. As an example, consider an action which is seen to be dishonest. If we analyse the action purely from the context of the action alone, presumably a dishonest act is always a dishonest act. But is there a difference when this act is performed by an honest person as compared to a dishonest person doing the same act? We could argue that an action is defined not only by a particular sequence of happenings but it also involves the quality of the person doing it. Institutions are very much based on this logic, particularly because there are very difficult decisions that an organisation has to make about its employees. It would be quite impossible to evaluate every action of the organisation towards all its employees in terms of 'good' and 'bad' action. For example, some organisations may be forced to lay off somebody or might not give a promotion to another. These acts cannot be evaluated in themselves and by themselves. What makes these decisions ethical or unethical is also dependent on the virtues of the organisation and the way these virtues are embodied in its rules and processes.

Another influential theory focuses on the ideas of duties and obligations. These theories are in principle non-consequentialist – that is, the value of the action is not evaluated by the consequences of that action. To give a simple real-life example: in one of the elections in Tamil Nadu, members of a political party went house to house in a particular area and distributed Rs 2000 for each voting member in that household. There were some who refused to take the money because the act in itself was seen as a corrupt practice, regardless of which party used it. There were many others who took the money and kept it for themselves. Still others took the money but gave it away to help others. How can we evaluate these actions? First is taking money for voting, which constitutes a corrupt act both for the person who is giving the money and the person who is taking the money. These acts can be understood through the framework of duty and of consequence. For the duty theorist, it is our duty not to accept the money, independent of what good we may do with it. For the consequentialist, taking the money is acceptable because we can do good as a consequence of taking the money.

Consequentialist theories are generally often invoked in discussions of ethics. Simply put, an action is morally correct if its consequences are favourable. But favourable to whom? I might act in a manner that might favour me or might favour another person or maybe a larger community. Consequentialist theories discuss these different kinds of consequences. If an action is such that its consequence is favourable to the person performing that action then it is the libertarian view; if it is favourable to everyone else but not the person doing that action it is called altruism, and finally if it is favourable to 'everybody' then it is called utilitarianism. So an action is evaluated through the consequences of that action to different segments.

In discussions of ethical actions of governments, we often hear the 'greatest good' argument. This view, which is a form of utilitarianism, holds that an action is morally right if the largest number of people benefit from it. Almost all actions by the State are justified by this argument. A dam displaces many and causes untold suffering to a segment of the population. Yet, building a dam may be seen to be ethically correct since it benefits more people than those who suffer because of it. This has become so much of a de facto argument these days that the nuances of this position seem to have been lost on those who use this argument repeatedly.

Another approach that is also much invoked in the public domain is the view of ethics based on rights – natural and human rights. In India today, the right to information, to education, to health, to food, to work etc. have had important consequences. In the context of philanthropy, we can ask whether there is a right for the marginalised and dispossessed that they should be helped by those who are better off. If not by individuals, does the society at least have a duty to help the poor? Or equivalently, do the poor have a right vis-à-vis the wider society to have a better life? The right to education, to food and suchlike are attempts to use the language of rights to redress the imbalance. However, one does not have to necessarily use the language of rights to address this inequality. Sometimes it may be better to invoke the notion of care as a moral category. Care ethics, which has become more popular in recent times and is commonly associated with what has come to be called 'feminist ethics', is a formulation that focuses on the importance of care (such as in care-giving) as ethical action. To understand philanthropic action, care may be more useful than the language of rights. Philanthropists give to the needy not because they think that the needy have a right to their money but because of more complex reasons that involve notions such as care, empathy, duty and humanity.

The Indian context: some examples

What I have tried to do here is to give an outline of some concepts, principles and theories in ethics. However, there is a problem in such a generalised approach to ethics. In the practical world, many often react impatiently when they hear these theories about ethics, especially when their main concern is to resolve an ethical crisis. Many times they are not even aware that there is an ethical problem in a given situation. They often find that ethical questions end up as long justifications of different positions, at the end of which they find that there is no clear direction on the next step of action. However, ethical analysis in general cannot be like an agony aunt column, where a 'specialist' on ethics will give specific suggestions on what to do. Ethical thinking requires working through these questions and taking the best decision in the particular context of the problem. To be able to do this, one has to know how to think through the problem in terms of the various ethical issues involved in it. Thus, some of the themes discussed above can function as general guidelines to take the discussion further instead of merely saying 'I think this is right' and somebody else saying 'No, I think this is right'. Engaging with ethics is a way to create meaningful and reasonable discussions within an organisation so that there is a more effective and ethical approach to all decision making, especially those decisions that affect other people and the wider society. There are no global prescriptions either since ethical responses depend deeply on the local contexts. It is for this reason that we cannot blindly follow the approaches to ethics that have been developed for the dominant western societies. The Indian context raises many new and complex questions of ethics in all domains, including business, education and medicine. In this section, I will consider some unique challenges that arise in the Indian context.

Ethical issues that are of relevance to business and philanthropy are primarily those associated with ethics related to institutions such as matters of governance, financial probity and management of employees. The Indian case offers unique challenges to the incorporation of ethics within this broader organisational structure. This problem is endemic across types of institutions ranging from pure business organisations to academic institutions and even smaller NGOs. Modern corporations tend to follow financial and accounting norms that are expected of them in the global world but in the case of formulating and following ethical norms there is a different mindset.

Sociologically, one can relate the nature of institutions in India to the importance of the image of the family. This image of the family is supported by the image of the patriarchal figure, the head of the family. Often the relationship between the head of an organisation and the employees is filtered through the language of family. The repeated use of the slogan by heads of organisations – 'we are a family' – adds a literal sense to this powerful idea of the family that influences organisational behaviour. One of the major drawbacks of the persistence of the model of the family is that loyalty and patronage become the norms of everyday practice in these institutions. This breeds a culture of sycophancy and lack of professional accountability for almost anything that happens in an organisation. This is true of schools and universities, as well as national research institutes and of multinationals. It is true of the social sector in the many NGOs which mediate between the funders and the community.

Due to the unique caste equation within Indian society, businesses are also dominantly run by families, often along caste lines. Even some of the biggest businesses in India, such as the Reliance group, arose as family businesses and even though they have become public entities the role of the family (and all that a family entails within the Indian context) still dominates. In the public imagination, many of these companies are seen primarily as family businesses. Small businesses are primarily distributed along family, caste and community lines across the country.

Why does this matter for an ethics of philanthropy? The most important aspect of philanthropy is the institutionalisation and professionalisation of giving money for non-business purposes. Many of the small family-run businesses in India donate money for various causes, primarily those that are related to their religion and community. Some support hospitals and education. However, the model that drives this giving is primarily that of charity. The important difference between charity and philanthropy really lies in the responsibility and accountability that philanthropy demands. Unlike charity where people believe that they are doing good by donating money without having a sense of accountability, philanthropic acts are answerable to a host of agencies including the government and the wider society. So where some of these companies have started philanthropy wings they take care of what they consider as the most important component of accountability – the accounts. It is financial accountability that has become the norm for almost all these philanthropy organisations, but this is at the expense of some basic ethical norms expected of philanthropy. The family business model only adds to this problem.

Not all business corporations have such close ties to family nor is the family the goal of many of these concerns. When we look at business corporations that have a strong and independent wing of philanthropy, we can begin with the Tatas. The Tatas have a long history of professional philanthropy for over a hundred years. The desire of a unified and prosperous nation was part of their vision of philanthropy. But many of the new entrants to this field, including IT giants like Wipro and Infosys, do not come from the perspective which catalysed the Tatas in the beginning. And this is to be expected since the context in which philanthropy is operating now is very different than pre-Independence times. So if we see what these new players are doing in the field of philanthropy we can see clear patterns of social intervention. The Tatas have a reputation for supporting education, health and also the arts. Their support to the arts expanded the notion of philanthropy and showed how philanthropy could be expanded beyond mere economic well-being. Among the newer organisations (and increasingly within the Tatas), support for art as a philanthropic activity is much less than what it should ideally be and philanthropy is now more conservatively viewed in terms of poverty and development. In particular, what also distinguishes this growing intervention by the philanthropists in India today is a strong belief in the use of new technologies to resolve social issues, whether it is the use of computers in classrooms or the use of satellites for agriculture.

Specific challenges in the Indian context

It is important to recognise the kind of responses towards these philanthropic initiatives, both from the people who are beneficiaries and those who are doing the work on the ground with these people. It is useful to list these responses so that we are aware of some blind spots in philanthropy. I do not necessarily agree with all the criticisms but do believe that it is necessary for the philanthropists to be more aware of these issues and factor them into their philanthropic initiatives. Some would also argue that the critique of the philanthropic organisations are from people and NGOs who want to retain the status quo and are resistant to certain kinds of change. I will not make a judgement on this debate except to point out certain examples which may be illustrative of the way forward and also to show how these problems are largely related to ethics.

Social vision of the philanthropist and the key decision makers

One major criticism of Indian philanthropy has been the role of the views of the founder and other dominant members of the philanthropic organisation. In philanthropistic organisations which have the presence of the founder, the founder's views tend to dominate thereby forcing the organisation to deliver what the founder and the founder's family understand as social change. Themes for philanthropic work then depend on what these people consider as important and how the intervention must be done on the ground. In principle, this is based on the view that the person who foots the bill and gives the money has a right to expect what they want done with that money. However, in philanthropy such an argument can be a problem since the impact of the intervention is not on their business but on the people and community. So, when the funders and their representatives make decisions based on their opinions or beliefs about the society then there is an ethical issue. One would hope then that these philanthropists will hire competent people to not just follow their bidding but also to properly advise them on the impact of their social intervention. However, what often happens is that people close to the parent organisation are chosen to run the philanthropic organisations. Often, there is a quick translation from a person's capacity to run a business to taking care of the problems of society, but many times these capacities are not transferable! This is similar to the government's propensity to hire scientists, who are experts in their particular domains, to advise the government on everything ranging from poverty alleviation to international diplomacy! The fact that the business tycoons have the power to intervene in ways that they think are 'correct' has less to do with the correctness of their vision and more to do with the money they are willing to give.

Field and domain knowledge versus modern management techniques

A related complaint about Indian philanthropy from those who work on the ground, including the beneficiaries, is related to the employees of philanthropic organisations. The notion of 'competent advisors/employees' has become a contentious issue in philanthropy. In the name of professionally running these organisations, there are many MBAs and those from the corporate world who now occupy leadership and decision-making positions in these organisations. In principle, there is nothing wrong with this for after all any organisation will be effective when it is managed professionally. However, what are the expectations and skill sets needed of a person working in the social sector field? Can they be responsible for decisions without an adequate understanding of society, social processes, the nature of political action etc.? Is competence in finance or engineering enough to take on this role? One of the common complaints from NGOs that have worked for decades in the field is that many times the representatives of the philanthropic organisation, who come with little understanding of the social situation or the work people have already been doing in these places, will dictate what has to be done. Since there are huge amounts involved, often the NGOs keep quiet. This attitude compromises both the philanthropic act as well as the NGOs which struggle to survive doing social work.

Pet theories and pet solutions

When philanthropic organisations attempt to solve problems in societies as understood by them then we end up with more problems. Some groups who thought technology is a solution for problems in education or trading of commodities (including vegetables and fish) dumped technologies on communities which were not prepared, or did not have the infrastructure, to engage with these technologies. In education, other such problematic interventions abound. For example, the philanthropic organisations related to Infosys and Mahindra have donated significant amounts of money to support educational/research programmes in universities in the UK and the US. Similar support to Indian universities is not so easily forthcoming from these or other organisations. Infosys has an organic connection to Bangalore but critics have pointed out that its support to the student community in the humanities (in which a disproportionate amount of marginalised students also study) in the three universities in Bangalore is quite dismal while their support to humanities in western universities is quite significant. A famous contemporary dance festival, which is closely linked to the use of digital technology, survives with great difficulty every two years in Bangalore but has had little support from the IT companies in Bangalore, the so-called IT capital of India, including Infosys. (Moreover, many arts organisations, when funded by such institutions, have to follow absurd demands ranging from how long an artist can perform to who should be invited.)

There is a deep impact on Indian higher education due to these philanthropic acts by some of these organisations, one of which is that it continues to promote western academics as the hope for those in India. Given that humanities education in India suffers from a great problem of quality education, donating millions of dollars to establish centres, Chairs and publishing grants housed in western universities accomplishes two things: firstly, it demoralises and erodes humanities education within India and secondly, it perpetuates the myth that the best academic work is that which is produced outside India, even if it is work on India and its traditions! This obsession about donating money to foreign universities, particularly when there is such a crisis within Indian education, is quite symptomatic of their broader worldview. For example, the Infosys Prize continues to have juries that are primarily composed of those working abroad and through this act they perpetuate beliefs about the impossibility of Indians to recognise merit of their own and various other related prejudices about work being done in India. It gets its prestige because of the huge prize amount as well as its association with 'Indians' living abroad who act as the jury. There are many such examples. A student of mine who went to the US to study got funds from the US to learn Kannada in Mysore but such support is almost impossible to get in India for students studying here from our philanthropic organisations.

Philanthropic organisations in India are deeply invested in education. The Tatas have helped set up institutes like the Indian Institute of Science and the Tata Institute of the Social Sciences. New entrants like Azim Premji and Shiv Nadar have started full-blown universities, with special support for the humanities and liberal arts. Although the universities (bearing the names of these two individuals) charge fees for students, there is a large amount of money spent as philanthropy to establish these universities. But even in the case of these educational initiatives, there is a significant top-down approach to what education should be. This is largely driven not just by the vision of a small group of people at the top but is also influenced by management strategies drawn from the corporate world. This has led to some conflict but overall I do believe that this is going to be the preferred model of the government and the private sector in India. The problems arising from corporates running universities is related to the problem about job requirements for philanthropy that was mentioned above. Ironically, the justification for private universities is based on the problems of government-run universities, such as patronage of the politicians in choosing the Vice-Chancellors or the problems that the faculty face or the sacrifice of academic merit for loyalty and patronage, and the lack of opportunity for students to study. However, in many of the private initiatives in education in India, including universities and research institutions, very similar practices are followed by the private groups. The leadership in these institutions are primarily those who are trusted by the funders. There is little job security, evaluations are often 'fixed', there is no space for disagreement on policies, the fee structure is so high that extremely few can afford to pay it, and so on.

Philanthropy and suspicion

Philanthropy in India is in this odd situation: foreign philanthropic institutions fund a range of activities which are not only about the poor and the vulnerable, such as support for the arts in various ways, student scholarship, heritage conservation and protection of certain cultural forms. It is difficult to get Indian organisations to support such important initiatives within the country (with exceptions like the Tatas earlier) and there are many examples where important cultural forms (including Indian texts, libraries and heritage buildings) have been protected by foreign funds when no Indian organisation had come forward to support them. An important reason for this is the inherent suspicion that the funders have about the way 'their' money is used by the fundees. There are two levels of suspicion in Indian philanthropy: the first is the suspicion (and many times disdain) of the government and the second is the suspicion that their 'hard-earned' money will be squandered by those who are receiving support. The role of suspicion distinguishes charity and philanthropy. Many times when people give money away as charity, they are not really holding the beneficiaries to any form of accountability. In philanthropy today, the beneficiaries have to constantly 'prove' that they are honestly using the funds and this wider mood of suspicion has turned a lot of people away from approaching these funders. We have found many groups working in the social sector and in the arts who feel that funders look upon them always with suspicion. Since suspicion is really about the money, there is excessive focus on auditing and accounting procedures. When an NGO gets money from these corporate philanthropic organisations, they typically have to get the latest management and financial accounting systems. In order to get this done, they have to hire people with competence in these fields. These people do not work for the kind of salaries which are paid to the other social workers. This leads to a complete reworking of salary and management structures in these organisations. And the worst impact of all this happens when the funding is stopped after three or five years. The NGOs are left with all these systems and bloated salaries for which they cannot get funding! The excessive use of management and financial strategies are pushed onto the social workers as a way of making them more efficient. The success of such initiatives should be evaluated now since many of the NGOs either follow some of these rules ritualistically or opt out of being dominated by the funder.

The attitude of the philanthropists towards alleviating poverty is commendable but the mechanism is not. Since the organisations deal with the fundees as if the money they give is somehow 'ours' there is an inherent tension, an underlying sense of suspicion, in the act of giving. Beneficiaries of funds describe how many times the funders tell them how they should do their job and what they should do 'to'/'for' the people. The leadership of philanthropic organisations live in a world that is quite different from the domains they want to change. The people they hire to help them take these decisions are also rarely part of these groups who are the beneficiaries or working directly with the beneficiaries. A good illustration of this dissonance lies in the salaries of the employees in philanthropy organisations. It is well known that salary and administrative costs of many philanthropy organisations ranges from 70 to 80% of the total funds raised for, or allocated to, philanthropy. The salaries paid to their 'professional' employees are more comparable to the corporate structure of the parent business group. In the social sector, there is a huge disparity between salaries, payments and expenditures of employees of the philan-thropic organisation and that of the salaries of the fundees and the beneficiaries. More worrisome is the fact that these employees have to take an empathetic and informed decision on the problem of the recipients and decide whether the approach they are funding is indeed the best one in the given circumstances. Since any help to the poor is a boon, the receivers of the funds often remain silent. What helps the philanthropists in this view is the decline of the welfare state and the growth of the power of the corporates. Through philanthropy, these private, business organisations play the role of politicians and administrators but without the accountability that regulates government administrators.

These tendencies illustrate the underlying belief about philanthropy in India. The belief that funding arts is a luxury, that giving money to our public universities and schools is a 'waste', and the belief that because they give the money they can do what they want without any explicit ethical code of conduct exemplifies the fundamental approach to philanthropy by these philanthropists.

We should remember that institutionalised philanthropy intervenes not only in individual lives but also in larger communities. Actions of philanthropy have an effect on social practices and social structures. They obviously can help people but they can also have consequences that are not desirable. Should a funder evaluate all these possibilities before deciding on support to their fundees? But will too much analysis cause paralysis of action and lead to a situation where philanthropy becomes more of a burden? We are in a situation today where some organisations have more money than they can disburse and so there is a pressure to disburse money. The specific issues discussed above include the enduring problem of what happens to the fundee and the community when the funder withdraws. As mentioned above, some funders give good salaries, and expect the latest financial software packages and digital management. However, what happens when the funder ends that support? Many philanthropic organisations do not want to be put in a situation where they continue to keep funding any particular organisation for a long time. Thus, they have requirements where the fundee has to raise funds from other sources for their projects. But in a place where there are very few big-time players, it is difficult to get equivalent funds from other funders. So what happens to the people and the community who have benefitted from the funding? It is surprising how much residual bitterness is present among those organisations which have been funded for a few years and then dropped from funding due to the view that philanthropists do not want to keep funding an organisation beyond a fixed time frame. It has also had an effect on the impact of their work on the ground and on the people and communities they have been working with.

Furthermore, there are deeper issues of accountability. Funders enter into the social sector genuinely wanting to do good and make a difference to the abject living conditions of the poor and marginalised. However, the people who manage the funds are most often not from the field areas. Typically in India, the majority of people who work in the major philanthropic organisations are urban, English educated and well off. Should they be expected to have certain kinds of training before they make decisions that can change people's lives and social dynamics? The government officials who are involved in similar interventions come with a different training, experience and background. This does not make them better employees but in the case of government employees there is a sense of transparency and public accountability. On the other hand, private philanthropists enter into these domains only because the government has miserably failed to provide a basic dignified health service, education and other necessary social amenities. So the main question is the nature of accountability applicable to philanthropists. In the name of doing a 'good' act, can they get away with doing anything? Can they be held responsible for any of their decisions?

There is a parallel in medical ethics that illustrates this problem. Many hospitals give medicines, and sometimes other facilities, for free to poor patients who cannot pay for these services. But just because they give these for free, can the doctors experiment with the patients as they like? Can they afford to test new drugs or do a procedure differently on these patients just because they are getting it for free due to their poverty? In principle, this cannot be done and the codes of medical ethics are ways to protect the patient from such abuse. Similarly, what is the minimum that we can and should expect from this 'free' distribution of wealth to the needy and others? Today, the only strong accountability that is followed, as mentioned earlier, by most of these philanthropic organisations is financial accountability – but this is more of a check to see if the funds are being utilised properly. This attitude has led to cases where the funders do not take a position on the unethical acts of an organisation as long as the accounting is done as required! Financial probity has replaced the more urgently needed sense of ethical codes applicable both to the fundee and the funder.

We only have to realise that wherever there is the presence of power, then there are bound to be ethical issues lurking around. The power in philanthropists comes from the money that they have, the money that they can distribute, the social capital in terms of their social standing, class, caste and many times gender, the organisational support they have, and the political ties and relations with the government that many of them have. An ethics of philanthropy is first and foremost an awareness of this power, self-regulation of this power, and the realisation that there should be some notion of accountability of this power when they use it to intervene in society.

While the points above give an idea of the complexity of philanthropy in India, it is necessary to realise the importance of philanthropy by the private sector. The enormous disparity in wealth, the lack of basic access to health and education, the lack of proper systems of justice across the country has led to a position where the private sector has to intervene in order to 'help out' the government. The government too, in general, has been open to such interventions and in some cases, like in the case of self-help groups in Tamil Nadu, the political parties and the government themselves enter into the social work sector. The problems mentioned above are only to highlight the importance of framing proper and broad ethical guidelines in philanthropy. These guidelines have to be sensitive to the nature of the social world and not be reduced only to certain management techniques. A philanthropic organisation cannot afford to be unaware of the complexities of class, caste, religion and gender in India while it intervenes in society since that would lead to serious ethical issues. On the other hand, ethics cannot be reduced to a checklist and a set of do's and don'ts. It needs sustained reflection and dialogue. Since there are no clear-cut solutions to ethical dilemmas, many people who confront these dilemmas end up taking decisions in the best way they can at that moment.

Thus, an ethics of philanthropy is first developed not by starting with a checklist but by finding ways to think through the concepts about the nature of 'helping', 'changing society', the meaning of private and public, volunteerism and so on. An ethical stance is one that will always challenge our cherished beliefs about many aspects of our social and personal lives. I believe that JRD Tata's approach to business is a good illustration of the complex ideas that underlie the act of philanthropy. I would even go to the extent of arguing that his approach to business is already responding to questions of philanthropy and that it is not really possible to remove philanthropy from his business practices. In a broader sense, I think it would be possible to say this of the Tatas historically, although I am not sure that such a vision is followed today or is even possible to be followed today.

In the chapters that follow, I will be exploring some key ideas that arise through JRD's writings. The themes that I discuss are not ones that I have imposed on him. The themes of these chapters arose from his own writings which showed an engagement with these terms. As mentioned in the previous chapter, these writings were accessed in the archives of JRD, both at Pune and Jamshedpur. So, in a sense, I am only acting as a voice that brings together some of these strands of thought in JRD's own reflections on his activities.

I am not discussing this conceptual world of JRD in terms of the activity of doing business. I believe that JRD's reflection on these themes very strongly exemplifies the point I made earlier about the intrinsic relation between philanthropy and business that I believe was integral to JRD's thinking about business. At the least, we can say that JRD's approach to business was sensitive to some of these concerns, although not always expressed or even understood as such.

I explore some of these core themes in the chapters that follow. The concepts that automatically arise in such ethical reflections on what to do with the profit one earns lead to concepts such as trusteeship, social responsibility, social audit, a more broader notion of the public and the private, as well as of profit itself. The point I am making is simple: if we want to answer the difficult ethical questions that arise in philanthropy, what we should be looking for in ethics is not a set of easy answers. Rather, what is needed is an awareness of the concepts that underlie our beliefs about business, profit, social responsibility and so on. To be ethical is to be ready to modify our conceptual world and accept changes to the standard ways of understanding concepts such as profit, private, public, ownership, social responsibility etc. The answers to ethical dilemmas need such conceptual changes and thus need some philosophical reflection. Perhaps the best example from the world of business of a person who rethought these concepts in fresh ways is JRD. The reason for this is because the question of philanthropy was an essential part of what it meant for him to be an entrepreneur and a leader.

Notes

1 For a relatively recent edited volume, see P. Illingworth, T. Pogge and L. Wenar (eds), 'Introduction', in *Giving Well: The Ethics of Philanthropy*. New York: Oxford University Press, 2011.

2 R. Menezes and S. Pandey. 'Q&A with Ratan Tata.' *Impact India 2*, Spring 2017, available at *Stanford Social Innovation Review*, https://ssir.org/articles/entry/qa_with_ratan_tata (accessed 10 January 2020).

3 For example, A. Santicola, 'Seven Ethical Challenges for Nonprofits', *NonProfit PRO*, 12 September 2006. Available at www.nonprofitpro.com/article/seven-ethical-challenges-nonprofits-36563/all/ (accessed 15 January 2020). See also D. L. Rhode and A. K. Packel, 'Ethics and Nonprofits', *Stanford Social Innovation Review*, Summer 2009. Available at https://ssir.org/articles/entry/ethics_and_nonprofits (accessed 15 January 2020).

3

TRUSTEESHIP[1]

Trusteeship is the model of responsibility that best describes JRD's view of himself and his role in the world. It was a view that JRD derived from Gandhi. This chapter begins with a short summary of the relationship between Gandhi and the Tatas, which began with Ratan Tata's monetary support to Gandhi's Satyagraha struggle in South Africa. Gandhi also visited Jamshedpur and by all accounts was pleased with the relation between labour and management there. But what really brought JRD and Gandhi together in spirit was the idea of trusteeship. Both of them lived by it in their personal lives and both demanded it of others.

Trusteeship is the view that one owns one's wealth only as a trustee on behalf of others. It is based on Gandhi's belief that one should not have more wealth than is really necessary. There are many important consequences of holding a position of trusteeship. There are also many serious problems. JRD did not formulate any theoretical description of trusteeship but his actions were mediated by his view of himself as a trustee of his, as well as his company's, wealth and resources. In the second section I discuss many of these issues associated with trusteeship as described by Gandhi. Following this, I look at JRD's attempts to create a mechanism of trusteeship. Here I think JRD's contribution to this subject is indeed very important. JRD chose voluntarily the path of trusteeship as far as his wealth was concerned. All his wealth was literally placed in a Trust, which is administered to support various activities. However, he also went one step further by demanding that his companies also act as trustees of the wealth they create. In doing so, he did not depend on the voluntary spirit of his employees to establish the spirit of trusteeship. Instead, what he did was to institutionalise social welfare programmes, thereby introducing some institutional mechanisms which would sustain the idea of trusteeship in his companies. Institutional mechanisms are extremely important because even in the absence of the individual with the original vision of trusteeship, its practice nevertheless gets supported, sustained and developed.

JRD's emphasis on institutionalisation and professionalisation were important departures from Gandhi's, and also more successful. This chapter concludes with a discussion of various programmes that illustrate the successful institutionalisation of the idea of trusteeship.

JRD and Gandhi

> Gandhiji, by far the greatest personality and, to this day, the most extraordinary human being I have ever met, inspired in me, as in most people, a mixture of awe, admiration and affection combined with some scepticism about his economic philosophy despite which one would follow or support him to the end, come what may. Perhaps the most endearing trait I found in him was his almost childlike sense of fun to which he gave vent in a chuckle which he sometimes used deliberately to put one at ease in his presence. He was also, like Jawaharlal Nehru, the most considerate and courteous of men who would never leave a question or a letter, however unimportant, unanswered.[2]

Gandhi's relation with the Tatas goes back to his days in South Africa. Sir Ratan Tata sent a letter along with a cheque of Rs 25,000 in 1909 in order to help Gandhi in his struggle against the apartheid government in South Africa. Over that year and the next, Gandhi received more such contributions from Ratan Tata to support Gandhi's Satyagraha movement in South Africa.

Gandhi also visited Jamshedpur more than once. In 1925, when he first visited that place, there was a meeting with the workers. In that meeting, Gandhi talked about identifying himself foremost as a labourer. He went to Jamshedpur mainly for the sake of the labourers. In the speech which he delivered during this trip, he made explicit his view of capitalists in relation to labour.

> I have always said that my ideal is that capital and labour should supplement and help each other. They should be a great family living in unity and harmony, capital not only looking to the material welfare of the labourers, but their moral welfare also – capitalists being trustees for the welfare of the labouring classes under them.[3]

In the same speech, he also reiterated that his 'identification with labour does not conflict with my friendship with capital.' He went on to add, 'And believe me, throughout my public service of 35 years, though I have been obliged to range myself seemingly against capital, capitalists have in the end regarded me as their true friend.' He said that he came as a friend of the Tatas and remembered with gratitude the support of Sir Ratan Tata to their struggle in South Africa.

What brought JRD and Gandhi together were two important facets of their worldview: that of trusteeship and their consistent concern for people less privileged than themselves, which included the labour class. The idea of trusteeship was very influential for JRD and he lived by his belief in this idea. We can see Gandhi's influence in this matter, an influence which JRD acknowledged in various places over the years. In a letter written in 1979, he wrote:

> I naturally agree with the sentiments you have expressed in your letters and your references to Bapuji's teachings and ideals, now so neglected. I do my best to live up to them in a true spirit of trusteeship in the conduct of such business as is within my responsibility.[4]

In the case of labour, both JRD and Gandhi were concerned with fundamental issues related to the welfare of labour. It is fair to say that JRD was a leader in labour welfare in the country, especially in the private sector. As mentioned earlier, many of the labour welfare schemes which he introduced in his companies were later incorporated by the government as labour laws.

However, JRD and Gandhi also differed sharply. JRD was particularly unhappy with Gandhi's economic ideas whereas Gandhi negatively reacted to a plan of some industrialists, including JRD, to tour England and the US, before independence, for better business prospects, a trip supported by the British rulers. Gandhi, for all his 'sympathy' with the business leaders, also expected a high ethical standard in business, a standard which most people did not measure up to. As was clear, it was not only people in business who could not measure up to the high personal ethical standards expected by Gandhi. However, there is a paradoxical tension between capitalism and Gandhi's worldview, one which placed him in potential conflict with an industrialist like JRD.

But what was important was that JRD, in spite of his misgivings about Gandhi's economic outlook, had the greatest respect for him and moreover was profoundly influenced by Gandhi's idea of trusteeship, which he followed in his own way. On many occasions, he explicitly noted that he functioned as a trustee and not as an owner in a pejorative sense of that word. Over the years, JRD projected the idea of trusteeship into the public domain, perhaps in the hope that it would be accepted, analysed and developed by other people, including the owners of other rich business enterprises.

Gandhi influenced many different kinds of people all over the world to follow or formulate some principles of trusteeship specific to their particular contexts. However, Gandhi's view of trusteeship was not accepted in general and even today it is found only in some isolated experiments. JRD's insistence on trusteeship may not have fared much better, especially his demand that private entrepreneurs and public servants such as bureaucrats understand their role as trustees.[5] I believe that JRD's idea of trusteeship was characterised more by its practice and implementation in a domain which had for long resisted any such move. To understand JRD's approach to trusteeship, it will be useful to analyse Gandhi's original idea of it.

Gandhi on trusteeship

> Supposing I have come by a fair amount of wealth – either by way of legacy, or by means of trade and industry – I must know that all that wealth does not belong to me; what belongs to me is the right to an honourable livelihood, no better than that enjoyed by millions of others. The rest of my wealth belongs to the community and must be used for the welfare of the community.[6]

One of the most important principles that Gandhi enunciated and lived by is the above expression of the idea of trusteeship. This principle has great potential for transforming the nature of society and ethical individual behaviour. It is based on the idea of autonomous choice as a vehicle for justice. In this sense, its strength is the non-violence intrinsically associated with voluntary action involved in trusteeship. In fact, Gandhi believed that his view on trusteeship would survive and had legitimacy because 'no other theory is compatible with non-violence.'[7] Moreover, this principle was based on an intrinsic notion of responsibility and duty going beyond personal gain. It is also a moderating principle in that it demanded a conscious decision to be made by individuals as to what (and how much) they really need to live a satisfied life. It is also important in the sense that it does not advocate sacrificing all the wealth but only to view one's wealth along the lines of trusteeship.

What was the basis for Gandhi to propose this form of 'economic governance' of one's wealth? We can discern one particular influence in his view that everything came from God. This, therefore, meant that what was given by God was meant for all and not for particular individuals. So, when an individual finds that she has more than her 'share' she should then see the surplus as strictly not belonging to herself. JRD did not explicitly subscribe to this particular theological view. To him, the nation or the larger society one belonged to would have been a substitute for God. JRD also laid strong emphasis on the individual's duty and responsibility towards trusteeship not because one's wealth was given by God but because that was the humane and ethical way of living, a view which is also in strong resonance with the larger Gandhian project of an ethical approach to living.

As we can see, there is a profound difference in the way one understands one's wealth in the context of trusteeship as against the standard view of ownership. Much hinges on how we understand ownership. Do we own our wealth? To answer this question, we need to understand the implication of ownership. For Gandhi and JRD, to own is to be a trustee, whereas in the normal connotation of the word, to own is to have freedom to do what one wants with it. To own as a trustee is to have responsibility over that wealth in that we are answerable as to how we spend it. It is this notion of answerability that distinguishes trusteeship over ownership. It is often, somewhat misguidedly, believed that to own is to be responsible only to oneself. This is part of a broader ethos where we understand the individual as being responsible for her deeds, good or bad. However, the sense of ownership as embodied as a trustee is the claim that we are accountable to something outside us, even when we spend our 'own' money.

This view of trusteeship leads to some serious problems, primarily about the role of those who are the owners of wealth and also about their incentive to continue to actively increase their wealth since they are accountable to various others. Regarding the owners of wealth, Gandhi said that they 'would be allowed to retain the stewardship of their possessions and to use their talent to increase the wealth, not for their own sakes, but for the sake of the nation and, therefore, without exploitation.'[8] There is already a problem in the claim that one is a trustee for the nation. What Gandhi meant by nation here was not the political rulers of the nation but its vast underbelly of underprivileged citizens. However, the State plays a very important role. According to Gandhi, the State would decide on what commission the trustees get based on their service! We can immediately see how this view would cause a potential conflict for JRD. Given the vagaries of the varying ideological position of the State, to let the State intervene in individual trusteeship would be potentially troublesome. However, Gandhi also noted that trusteeship should not be imposed from above, including the State, but must arise from below, from the people themselves, right from gram panchayats. There is also another indication of the suspicion that Gandhi had of the State's capacity to take over the stewardship of trustees. Gandhi believed that the State is 'a soulless machine' and had greater proclivity to violence.[9] Hence he preferred trusteeship based on an individual's own choice to administer his or her wealth for the poor rather than let the State take over this role.

It is clear that the owners of wealth must have a responsibility towards their wealth. There are two different kinds of responsibility which they should have. One is the responsibility of trusteeship, which is that they administer their wealth on behalf of others in the community and nation. The other responsibility is to increase their wealth, just as they would as if the wealth belonged exclusively for their personal use. In expecting this responsibility, Gandhi was expanding the meaning of profit to go beyond personal profit or personal material profit.

The latter responsibility that a trustee should increase their wealth leads to a problem. Since trusteeship is based on a moral foundation, there is a logical necessity that the means of attaining wealth as a trustee must also follow some ethical principles. Thus, this leads to the question about the means of earning this wealth. Gandhi repeatedly emphasised that we enjoy our wealth by renouncing it.[10] If this were so, then why would an individual create wealth if she were expected to renounce it? Furthermore, there is an added problem, one with its origin in almost all the ancient religions, which is that accumulation of wealth is often associated with 'impurity'. There is an added assumption, almost by default, that if one earns enormous amounts of money then this earning is definitely based on unfair means. In today's society, such a view is very much a part of the public imagination.

If this suspicion is present, then the issue that arises for trusteeship is about fair means of earning money and whether fair means, in principle, can generate appreciable increase in wealth. Reflecting this sentiment well, Shankarrao Deo wrote to Gandhi asking him to emphasise the importance of pure ways of making money. He wrote, 'If purity of means is strictly observed, then, according to me, crores could not be accumulated at all and the difficulty of spending for society will assume a very minor prospect.'[11]

However, Gandhi had two interesting responses to this question. One is that he wanted to make no judgement on people since 'who is to decide whether one is just or otherwise? And justice too is a relative term.'[12] His own personal action of renouncing his wealth was an example but Gandhi also said that just because he had renounced his wealth he could not demand that others do the same.[13] The second point he made was that it was always possible that somebody could discover (and thus 'inherit') wealth by finding gold or diamond on his or her land. More than this particular example, what is important to understand is the possibility of creating wealth without using unfair means. If there was anything that was central to JRD's philosophy of action, it was this emphasis on creating wealth without using unfair means.

There is always a tension between the nature of profiting and a just, proper way of profiting. As discussed earlier, there is a lurking feeling that one cannot create a large amount of wealth without indulging in some dishonest practice. The apocryphal story of Gandhi about the profitability of the Khadi enterprise is well known. It is said that when one of the owners of a Khadi enterprise claimed profit Gandhi was shaken because he believed that if that person had been honest, he would not have been able to make a profit! The popular belief that profiting is based on some form of exploitation manifests itself in ordinary discourse in various ways. But there is a way of understanding the possibility of profiting without necessarily accepting that large profits must be based on unfair practices. The term which can replace exploitation is cooperation. Gandhi believed that the 'rich cannot accumulate wealth without the cooperation of the poor in society.'[14] If every business act is understood in the spirit of cooperation and not of exploitation, then it is, in principle, possible to find ethical methods for increasing wealth.

The problem in this view is partly due to the positivistic approach of modern economic societies in which the individual becomes the ultimate unit. This then implies that the ownership of work done by an individual is seen to 'belong' to that individual alone. This also implies that what we are capable of earning is actually due to our own capacities and strengths. Once the individual (or equivalently, the group comprising the private, those who are the owners) is the privileged centre then the fruits of one's labours are seen to rightfully belong to that individual. However, this view runs counter to the simple observation that an individual reaches a status in her life due to a variety of factors, not least being the social capital she has access to. Thus, ownership and one's right to what they possess are complex issues. There is an obligation present in the act of owning, since the capacity to own something depends on various other factors, other than the individual. Even in the cases of individual creativity, where presumably the creative artist is the 'owner' of her artistic expression, the artist depends on material 'outside' her such as events in nature or society or in other people. Similarly, journalists depend on 'free' news but when they make that news theirs by copyright, they are essentially asserting their rights on something which was not really theirs to begin with.

While such a view (that ownership is never something that can belong only to one individual) may be somewhat true for the salaried and professional class, it is often remarked that many entrepreneurs have made something of themselves against all odds and with scarcely any support from any other person or any institution. However, this view is quite limited since there will always be factors outside the individual which allows the individual to succeed in any endeavour. Nevertheless, this view has become a part of our imagination. This is mainly because it reaches to the heart of the problem, which is when somebody, after all odds and constraints posed by the community and society, makes a success of her venture then what ethical duty does she have to pay back something to the larger society?

There is another dimension to the issue of unfair means that is not directly related to the generation of wealth but to those activities that are harmful in various ways. For example, as a trustee of the larger society, should companies refuse to indulge in not only unfair practices but in the creation of harmful products? Should they voluntarily abide by environmental safeguards? Not deal with governments and parties which are oppressive? Not work with technologies which may be unsafe and undesirable in various ways, including their use to support violence both at the individual and State level? And so on. Thus, the question of means which becomes paramount under the trusteeship view, and which is not overridden by concerns of private profit, places a greater social responsibility going beyond mere financial wealth.

So, for Gandhi, and to a great extent for JRD, the means to wealth is as important, if not more important, than the creation of wealth. Especially in the context of trusteeship, which involves taking a principled stand towards one's own wealth, there is a moral demand that the means by which that wealth is acquired should also be 'clean'. It is important to note that trusteeship of wealth is not restricted to material wealth. And trusteeship is not only a duty for the rich to perform. Even a labourer is a trustee of his 'wealth'. Gandhi mentioned that the 'labourer has to realise that the wealthy man is less owner of his wealth than the labourer is owner of *his* own, viz., the power to work.'[15] I believe that this is not only an important idea but one that has been lost in the excessive focus on material wealth. Firstly, what Gandhi was doing in claiming trusteeship for the labourer is to add value to the worth of the labourer. By so doing, he was negating the moral hierarchy that might mistakenly be attributed to trusteeship of material wealth over other forms of wealth. It is worthwhile noting that JRD's response to the welfare of the workers and his belief in the essential importance of workers to his organisation were also mediated by a belief and hope that the labourer would also be a trustee of that which is in his or her capacity.

There is another potential problem about trusteeship that is worth reflecting upon. It is often felt that when there is no incentive for material profit, an individual will lose the motivation to work harder and produce more profit. The idea of incentive has become the cornerstone of modern liberalisation. Incentives are seen as a reward for either doing excellent work in the job that is given to an individual or exceeding the expected output, and so on. Incentives do two things: firstly, it acknowledges that the individual has contributed to a greater share and secondly, it differentiates between people whose capabilities are different, including the capacity for hard work. It seems obvious, especially in a worldview where the autonomous individual is at the centre, that one who works more diligently and harder should be suitably rewarded. In fact, the very idea of leadership in business, for example, is based on the recognition of an individual's special strengths. Incentive is essential for business. If we ask what is the essential quality for business, it has to be something associated with incentive, since even profit is an incentive. This leads us to consider a troubling question: does trusteeship negate any incentive for developing one's wealth? Will the idea of trusteeship lead to a static worldview of business? One simple answer is that incentive should not be seen in terms of material difference alone. The essential point about incentive is the recognition of an individual's extra efforts, especially when others who *could* have done the same do not do so.

This should be a genuine worry for both Gandhi and JRD. In the case of JRD, it should be a greater source of worry since there is something similar in the idea of trusteeship and the Communist ideal. If there was anything that could annoy JRD immensely, it was the Communist system that supported what he called economic and political totalitarianism. It is commonly noted that the lack of incentive for individual growth in Communist societies played a great part in the demoralisation of the workforce. But, as is to be expected, both Gandhi and JRD do not expect a system based on trusteeship to also be one based on equality. Gandhi noted this explicitly when he wrote that we 'do not want to produce a dead equality where every person becomes or is rendered incapable of using his ability to the utmost possible extent. Such a society must ultimately perish'.[16] In other words, it is important to recognise a difference in the quality of individuals, at least in the capacity of individuals to be better in some kinds of work. The important point therefore is not that we do not recognise individual merit; rather, it is how this difference is rewarded or manifested. The fundamental issue is that between worth and reward. Even when we accept that one individual has contributed more to a particular initiative, it is still not clear what should be a just reward to acknowledge this effort. This is a problem that is not unique to business. Almost any organisation embodies this problem, whether it is a business concern, an academic institute or even a school.

Today, our globalised societies function as if one's worth is best acknowledged and rewarded through material incentives. There are also attempts to reward through positions of leadership, and even though they do not transform into material benefit they are sometimes seen to be more important, primarily because of the position of power. However, the dominant paradigm in today's world seems to be that of rewarding one's worth through material profit. Even the structure of salaries has been redesigned to exemplify this form of incentive to individuals. Thus, there is a genuine problem as to whether trusteeship implies a complete levelling of one's capabilities. In today's world where material wealth has become the standard for all comparisons, it seems obvious that a person with superior capability must be compensated only through material means. For Gandhi, the person with better ability in particular work should be allowed to do his or her best but the conversion of this difference in ability should not necessarily be in monetary terms. For JRD, this is also an important problem but one which he deals with quite differently.

The final point which I want to consider in Gandhi's notion of trusteeship is that of heirs. The question of heirs has been an age-old problem for human societies, especially in the context of ownership of wealth. If a person has some wealth, then when he dies who has the right to inherit it? By and large, with minor differences, almost all modern societies accept that an individual's wealth belongs to the family and therefore they have the first right to inherit it. The emphasis on the autonomy of the individual in societies meant that the individual had the right, through writing a will, for example, to choose his or her inheritors but the default mode is always the family. Cultural norms may also have been present in some cultures where primogeniture (inheritance by the eldest child, usually the eldest son) was the default mode.

The idea of trusteeship challenges this fundamental social belief and practice. If we are trustees to the wealth we possess, then it is ethically not ours to gift it to our family or children. Since trusteeship involves only being a trustee of one's wealth, we cannot bequeath it to anybody but the public. Gandhi repeatedly said that a 'trustee has no heir but the public.'[17] This meant that, if needed, the heir to a trustee should be one who in turn is best qualified as a trustee. Gandhi thought that the heir could be suggested by the trustee but had to be 'finalized by the State.'[18] The family has no stake in the wealth because once it is seen as being a Trust held on behalf of others then the family has anyway no right over it. Thus, who becomes the heir should really depend on the choice made by the trustee. However, the invocation of the State to finalise the heir is a problematic suggestion.

In the case of JRD and the Tatas, what is remarkable is that they have institutionalised the idea of trusteeship without using the agency of the State. The creation of different Trusts by the Tata leadership, including by Dorabji, Ratan Tata and JRD, is one mechanism of leaving their wealth to the public. In doing this, they were exhibiting the best spirit of trusteeship in that they viewed themselves as managing their personal wealth which was ultimately for the benefit of the public. The responsibility and accountability towards their wealth are also exhibited by their not living to the limits of the wealth they possessed and seeing their duty essentially as one of responsibility to the workers, community and even the country. The model of continued trusteeship in the Tatas is a model that draws upon Gandhi's vision but also goes beyond his emphasis on the role of the government. This model is also a useful one which shows how it is possible to act as trustees over generations through institutional mechanisms. In this respect, it is surprising that Gandhi felt that it was only Jamnalalji who came closest to his idea of a trustee.

For Gandhi, it was the State which had to step in to continue the role of trusteeship; for the Tatas it is their name, the weight of tradition and company policies that enable the continuity of their role as trustees. Those who are sympathetic to the idea of trusteeship and who are also suspicious of State intervention might do well to critically analyse this particular model of the Tatas. We should also remember that when Gandhi talked about the State he was quite concerned about the nature of the State since he believed that it was more aligned with violence than the individual. Further, in a clarification to the role of the State he explicitly said that he did not expect the State to confiscate private ownership in order to maintain trusteeship. In fact, he said that 'it was to avoid confiscation that the doctrine of trusteeship came into play retaining for the society the ability of the original owner in his own right'.[19]

Given Gandhi's pragmatism, it is to be expected that trusteeship was not to be seen as a theoretical formulation but one that was practically implementable. In fact, Gandhi approved a practical formula for trusteeship in 1942, which is given below. As we can see, this plan is only an outline and there are many details which need to be properly described and analysed.

1. Trusteeship provides a means of transforming the present capitalist order of society into an egalitarian one. It gives no quarter to capitalism, but gives the present owning class a chance of reforming itself. It is based on the faith that human nature is never beyond redemption.

2. It does not recognise any right of private ownership of property except so far as it may be permitted by society for its own welfare.

3. It does not exclude legislative regulation of the ownership and use of wealth.

4. Thus under State regulated trusteeship, an individual will not be free to hold or use his wealth for selfish satisfaction or in disregard of the interests of the society.

5. Just as it is proposed to fix a decent minimum living wage, even so a limit should be fixed for the maximum income that would be allowed to any person in society. The difference between such minimum and maximum incomes should be reasonable and equitable and variable from time to time so much so that the tendency would be towards obliteration of the difference.

6. Under the Gandhian economic order the character of production will be determined by social necessity and not by personal whim or greed.[20]

It should be clear that there are points in this proposal that JRD would have disagreed with. However, the problem about establishing working models of trusteeship only illustrates the complexity of this demand. JRD's approach is one particular model that tried to exhibit the possibility of living a life based on the idea of trusteeship, a model which, whether it follows all the Gandhian ideas or not, remains one of the most successful models to date.

Other approaches to trusteeship

Gandhi's idea of trusteeship is itself influenced by various religious traditions. The influence of *Gita* on Gandhi is well known and even in his utterances on trusteeship he draws upon the *Gita* and *Upanishads*, among other religious texts. In fact, the belief that all our wealth actually belongs to God is common to various texts including the *Gita* and *Isopanishad*. Among other religious traditions, Buddha too asked people to use their private property for the happiness of all and it was Jesus who asked a rich man to renounce his property and follow him. Islam too has a strong internal tradition of giving, many features of which are akin to the idea of trusteeship. Thus, in these traditions, we can see two universal responses to private wealth and ownership of that wealth. One is to renounce it and give it away as charity and the other is to nurture it and build on it but always with the responsibility as a trustee of that wealth.

Not only was Gandhi influenced by various doctrines that reflect some ideas of trusteeship but his emphasis on trusteeship has also spurred other organisations around the world to inculcate this ideal. Co-operatives, community ownership including that of water, newer management policies where the workers share a stake in the company, the recent institutionalisation of social audit and various indices related to non-profit issues are all instances which can be seen as experiments that share a common space with the idea of trusteeship. Not all or even some of them are inspired by Gandhi's writings but they are attempts to practically translate the ideal of trusteeship. In the Indian context, Vinobha Bhave was one who was not only drawn to this idea but also gave life to it through his own interpretations.[21] The Bhoodan and Gramadan movement of Vinobha were striking attempts to rethink the notion of private ownership.[22] Although in literature on trusteeship the name of JRD does not figure as it should, it is clear that his was one of the more successful attempts at trusteeship.

JRD and trusteeship

JRD was following a grand tradition of trusteeship, one that had already been initiated by Jamsetji Tata. Jamsetji was a pioneer not just in establishing new industries but also in his philanthropy. He had envisioned three great projects which he believed would be of great help to the nation. One was the production of steel, another was of power and the third was an academic institute. He partitioned his wealth into three parts towards this end, one of which was used to establish the Indian Institute of Science in Bangalore.

JRD acknowledged that the concept of trusteeship was conceived by Jamsetji Tata and that 'somehow the whole concept seemed to flow naturally from him.'[23] JRD in an interview in 1978 explained how the concept of trusteeship was so integral to their vision. If there is one company that has most publicly represented the Tatas over the decades it is their steel enterprise, TISCO (now called Tata Steel), based in Jamshedpur. Not only is the company synonymous with the Tatas but so also is the town. Although the total share of the Tatas in TISCO was only about 4% (as recorded in an interview in 1978), the dedication to the company by the Tatas is a reflection of the idea of trusteeship. In this context JRD said in the interview, 'We were merely leading and managing and sponsoring what we felt, in the totality of the various companies, was a large national enterprise'. Thus, this goes back to Jamsetji's vision of industrialising India, based on his belief that independence could be obtained and sustained only by being economically strong. Hence, their commitment to basic industries, those that would help build the nation, was 'almost treated as a national duty.'

JRD pointed out that even the managing agency system was owned 80 to 85% by public charity trusts.

> Therefore, the Tatas are in fact a Trust and an institution more than just a business house… right from the early days I knew Mahatma Gandhi and I was quite impressed and believed in the spirit of trusteeship. Not the spirit which has been sought to be formalised with no success up to now but one which, I think, has no need to be formalised. This, I think, is being done in our own House, naturally, because of our inheritance and the fact that we are owned by the trust. I think that is the best way to apply the spirit of trusteeship – to act as trustees and to consider the major problems of the country in connection with the operations of the firm as trustees and not as businessmen merely trying to make money for the firm. Incidentally, we want to make money, because that is the only way to make funds available for charitable trusts.[24]

It is clear that JRD's view of business can be far better understood when he is seen not just as a businessman with a conscience but more as a human being finding ways to function as a trustee of his capital. In a letter written in 1973 he explained in some detail his attempt to live up to the ideals of trusteeship. He wrote:

> I may say that I have always been basically in agreement with Gandhi's concept of trusteeship and have throughout my career tried to live up to it. In fact, our group of companies have, to the extent possible, officially adopted it as part of their credo. As I told you when we met, my only doubts have been in regard to the practical effect that can be given to such a concept, particularly considering, on the one hand, the ethical standards, or lack of them, that seem to prevail today amongst large sections of the business community of our country, and on the other, the dogmatic view of socialism and the resultant hostility towards private enterprise adopted by our government.
>
> I have again and again over the last few years publicly urged leaders of the business community to recognise its social responsibilities and to use such authority or economic power as they may have as Trustees. I would, therefore, be only too happy if some practical way were found of bringing the somewhat metaphysical concept of trusteeship in business closer to down to earth realities and needs of business and industrial organisation.[25]

It is indeed difficult to convert an idea into action. As JRD rightly notes, the 'metaphysical' concept of trusteeship is particularly difficult since it is associated with a host of problems in practice. Furthermore, Gandhi's ideas about trusteeship were actually not fully fleshed out. In fact, the draft proposal of the trusteeship formula, mentioned a few pages earlier, was published only in 1952, although Gandhi saw the draft and made some changes to it. From what JRD himself says in his speeches and writings, it is clear that he was very much influenced by this idea although he may have attempted to find his own ways of making it practicable. It would be useful to understand the pioneering innovations regarding labour and in general corporate responsibility, not just to the company and its employees, but also to the township and its surrounding communities as the influence of the idea of trusteeship.

In what follows, I will analyse various elements that are necessary to have a workable concept of trusteeship, especially as put into practice by JRD and his team. But most importantly, it is worthwhile noting that JRD tried to live by what he preached, in a sense similar to what Gandhi did. This is best exemplified by the Trusts into which all his personal wealth was gifted, following the grand tradition of the various Tata members establishing their Trusts such as the Sir Dorabji Tata Trust, Sir Ratan Tata Trust and others. And as an example of living a spartan life, spartan as compared to the total wealth he had at his command, we only need to look at his personal worth. Even as late as 1985, in response to an article which misquoted his wealth, JRD wrote a letter to the Editor of *Bombay* in which he added that the 'fact is that my wife's and my personal investments (including an apartment), were valued as on 31st March 1985 at less than Rs. 60 lakhs. All other shares stand in my name, amongst others, only as a trustee of public charitable trusts in which I obviously have no personal interest.'[26]

Not only did JRD leave his personal wealth for the public but he also tried to live by the spirit of trusteeship. There is yet another facet of his life that also reflects this spirit. This was not about wealth but about duty to the nation. When Tata Airlines was nationalised, JRD lost something which was very dear to him. But when he accepted the post of Chairman of Air-India he worked tirelessly to build its reputation as one of the finest airlines in the world. With his trademark meticulous attention to detail and efficiency, Air-India did indeed represent a new face of growing India. Moreover, his involvement in this government organisation was so much that he was sometimes accused of neglecting his own business! Among the many achievements in his life, including expanding the Tata group during his tenure as Chairman of the group, he was most proud of his stint at Air-India. He has gone on record saying that his 'proudest achievement' was Air-India. He was proud of it being a national asset – at least in his lifetime. His experience with Air-India is another illustration of trusteeship in action. JRD was not just placing his wealth for the public but he was also placing himself and his personal capabilities at the service of the nation, perhaps even at the expense of his own 'private' companies.

In a letter to a Professor at the Indian Institute of Management, Bangalore, he succinctly summarised the effect of trusteeship on his action. He wrote:

> If I were to attribute any single reason to such success as I have achieved, I would say that success would not have been possible without a sustained belief that what I did or attempted to do would serve the needs and interests of our country and our people and that I was a trustee of such interests.[27]

Institutionalising trusteeship

However, the most important contribution of JRD to the idea of trusteeship was not merely in his personal action. Like Gandhi, who believed that his personal behaviour would inspire others to follow, JRD too lived the spirit of trusteeship. But however much his personal practice is important, what is probably more significant is his attempt to institutionalise mechanisms that are related to trusteeship. As we saw earlier, even in the draft plan accepted by Gandhi, the six points were basically guidelines. The exact mechanism for implementation of these points was not explained. What JRD did was to establish ways of implementing some fundamental concepts related to trusteeship for private companies.

The Tatas have had a great impact on the people associated with them. A good relation with their employees can be explained by the fact that they are good employers and so there is no need to invoke the notion of trusteeship. However, their impact goes much beyond their immediate employees and this has happened primarily through the many Trusts established by them. These Trusts have benefitted people across the country, in the urban and rural sectors, independent of considerations such as religion, caste etc. The establishment of these Trusts where the personal wealth of these people is meant for utilisation for public service is one of the strongest signs of a dynamic concept of trusteeship. And what is important to note is that these Trusts are not seen as being merely charitable Trusts. In the foreword to Lala's book *The Heartbeat of a Trust*, JRD wrote that the 'tradition of Tata philanthropy was set by Jamsetji, the Founder of the House. The grand vision was his. To his sons, Dorabji and Ratan, and his cousin, R. D. Tata, goes the credit of continuing the tradition.'[28] What he didn't say here was that JRD placed all his wealth in a Trust which carries his name and is called the JRD Trust, which he set up in 1944.

JRD made a distinction between charity and philanthropy. Charity he saw as being static whereas trusteeship was more dynamic. Philanthropy, he wrote in the same foreword, 'has a more profound meaning than that of mere charity' since it means 'love of mankind'. He continued that 'when that love prevails, wealth assumes a nobler purpose'. He realised that in our nation there are a large number of people living in dire poverty and the trustees are therefore torn between responding to immediate problems or enabling programmes with long-term benefits. Although the Trusts do support solutions of short-term needs, their main concern has been to establish mechanisms that will enable a greater good for a greater number of people for greater time. In this context, grants towards education have been identified as one of the thrust areas.

These Trusts have also been involved in the creation of many pioneering institutions. The remarkable aspect of this is that after these institutions are set up and running, they are dedicated to the nation and become national properties. These institutions when given as a gift to the country had already established themselves as world-class ones. The expenditure and care taken to establish and nurture these institutions bears the special stamp of the Tatas. The roll call of these institutions is itself impressive: Tata Memorial Hospital for Cancer Research and Treatment, Tata Institute of Fundamental Research, Tata Institute of Social Sciences, National Centre for Performing Arts and National Institute of Advanced Studies. Earlier, Jamsetji was instrumental in establishing the Indian Institute of Science. The final line by JRD in the Foreword summarises well his view of practical trusteeship. JRD noted that their contribution may have been quantitatively small, especially in comparison to what needs to be done in the country, but hoped that it was 'qualitatively significant' and 'that in handling the wealth placed in our hands we fulfilled the vision and aims of Jamsetji Tata and his sons that this wealth which came from the people should go back to the people many times over'. These words were written in 1984 and over the last two decades many more new programmes are being supported by these Trusts and also by the companies belonging to the Tata group. The essence of a dynamic notion of trusteeship is captured in the belief that the wealth of these companies 'came from the people' and that it 'should go back to the people many times over'.

One of the greatest challenges facing the concept of trusteeship is posed by the private business enterprises. We have already discussed various aspects related to profit, individual autonomy and so on. The historical view of private ownership has always been strongly correlated with profiting for oneself or for the immediate owners. Even Gandhi's description of trusteeship is unclear as far as the mechanisms of trusteeship of private industrialists is concerned. An idealised view of trusteeship may be impractical. A mature practical approach towards trusteeship can only come from smaller experiments, whose lessons can help point to the potential problems and solutions in implementing this idea.

JRD's attempts to introduce various measures that immensely benefitted the labour sector should also be seen as one manifestation of the view of trusteeship. Right from the beginning, labour welfare was given prime importance in the steel factory. In 1912, an eight-hour working day was introduced in the factory before such a measure was introduced anywhere else in the world. JRD saw the importance of labour welfare and introduced a series of measures for their benefit and as early as 1947 started the Personnel Department. It is important to realise that this was not done under pressure of strike or conflict; after all, TISCO is remembered for the harmony between management and workers. JRD believed that the welfare of the workers was the welfare of the company and went beyond the call of duty, as understood in the capitalist enterprise, to establish a human relation based on empathy with the workers. This attitude reflects trusteeship in action. It is worth noting that many of these measures were made into laws by the Indian government long after their implementation by the Tatas. So also, some of these measures such as the eight-hour working day and leave with pay became statutory in many Western countries long after their introduction by the Tatas. A summary of these measures with a comparison of implementation dates in TISCO and by the government is given below.

- Eight-hour working day, introduced in TISCO in 1912 and enforced by law in 1948.
- Free medical aid, TISCO 1915, law 1948.
- Establishment of Welfare Department, TISCO 1917, law 1948.
- Schooling facilities for children, TISCO 1917, still not a law.
- Formation of Works Committee for handling complaints concerning service conditions and grievances, TISCO 1919, law 1947.
- Leave with pay, TISCO 1920, law 1948.
- Workers' Provident Fund Scheme, TISCO 1920, law 1952.
- Workmen's Accident Compensation Scheme, TISCO 1920, law 1924.
- Technical institute for training of apprentices, craftsmen and engineering graduates, TISCO 1921, law 1961.
- Maternity Benefit Act, TISCO 1928, law 1946.
- Profit Sharing Bonus, TISCO 1934, law 1965.
- Retiring Gratuity Act, TISCO 1937, law 1972.
- Ex-gratia payment – road accident while coming to or returning from duty, TISCO 1979, not yet law.
- Social audit, TISCO 1980, not yet law.
- Pension scheme, TISCO 1989, not yet law.

For JRD's notion of trusteeship, this concern for their employees must be extended to the larger society. JRD emphasised the importance of involving the company and its employees in various development projects for communities around Jamshedpur. This involved education as well as health programmes. Given that Jamshedpur falls in a tribal area, with a significant proportion of tribal population, JRD initiated a series of programmes designed for the tribal community. The institutionalisation of trusteeship was thus manifested in the creation of three departments under Tata Steel whose sole responsibility is social welfare in the urban, periurban and rural areas around Jamshedpur.

It is worth exploring the contours of these programmes because I believe that they exhibit one useful model to explain how trusteeship can be institutionalised in private concerns. Tata Steel has three separate departments dealing with social service: The Community Development & Social Welfare (CD&SW), and Rural & Tribal Services Division and Centre for Family Initiatives (CFI). These divisions also have associated societies that are autonomous and these are the Tata Steel Rural Development Society (TSRDS) and Tribal Cultural Society (TCS) promoted by Tata Steel. TSRDS was started in 1979 at the initiative of JRD. A special group to deal with tribals was formed as the Tribal Cultural Society and was registered as a society in 1993. TSRDS, for example, has a programme of mobile clinics which travel hundreds of kilometres every day to dispense medical help to various rural communities. These clinics dispense basic medicines as well as cater for the prevention and cure of diseases such as tuberculosis and leprosy. Mention must be made of the unique hospital on rails called the Lifeline Express. With the help of other organisations, TSRDS has sponsored this mobile hospital many times over the last decade. This train has all the facilities of a well-endowed major hospital and at a pre-announced time it visits a particular station. People all around that area access medical help with professional doctors on the train. An elaborate structure dependent on a grassroots network identifies patients and matches them with the ailments that can be treated on the train. The treatment is given in principle at no cost but if there are people who can donate something they are encouraged to do so.

Similarly, education is a sector where these groups do pioneering work at the ground level. Many schools and one college are supported by the Education Department as well as the Tribal Services group. TSRDS and TCS have supported infrastructural improvement in over 300 schools in the rural and *bustee* areas. The company also awards educational scholarships amounting to over 60 lakhs with special focus on SC and ST students. This includes special training where needed. Training schemes for employment are an integral part of these rural development programmes. The focus here is on enabling income generation from activities such as poultry farming, Durrie weaving, embroidery etc. Another important activity is the creation and support of *pani* panchayats where water management at the panchayat level has led to great benefits. Other than special fellowships for education and sports, special programmes for supporting tribal welfare include the establishment of a Tribal Culture Centre. This Centre has a heritage hall, which is a museum detailing various aspects of tribal life and culture. The Centre offers a place to support tribal activities including art and education.

The support to sports by the Tatas is well known. Dorabji was not only the first President of the Indian Olympic association in 1919 but he also sponsored four athletes and two wrestlers at the 1920 Olympics. Thus, it should not be a surprise that many international athletes and sportspersons in the country owe their growth to the Tatas. In recent times, special attention is on athletics and archery. In the case of archery, students are given a fellowship to stay in the sports academy and are rigorously trained under the guidance of both Indian and foreign coaches. As described earlier, the Tata Football Academy is one of the most successful experiments in developing football talent in the country. Again, this is an academy which is entirely supported by the company and has renowned coaches and other support systems such as modern nutritional catering and a specialist sports doctor in attendance. This residential programme, other than not taking fees from the students, offers free board and lodging, along with a monthly stipend, free playing kits and so on. These students also attend local schools during their training in the Academy.

A significant amount of funds is available for these activities. Similarly, the Tata-run hospital in Jamshedpur caters for both employees and non-employees. The magnificent parks under the company's care are as much a public property for locals and for visitors to Jamshedpur. The maintenance of the city is now under a separate corporate wing of the Tatas. These activities are supported by Tata Steel. Similarly, other Tata companies have their own outreach programmes. All these efforts attest to the practical success of JRD's vision of trusteeship.

The Tata vision of trusteeship is clearly seen in the way Jamshedpur is maintained and managed. Although Jamsetji did not live to see the town grow, he had a vision for it, a vision which dreamt of a town with broad roads, parks and areas for football and other games. Even though there was really no need to take on the responsibility of maintaining a town with high standards of urban management, the Tatas decided to do so. Jamshedpur is a model town in many ways. JRD's involvement with this town, although he spent little time there, is illustrative of his view of himself as a trustee, among other things a trustee of this town. An ex-resident of Jamshedpur, who visited the city on a visit, wrote to JRD in 1987 about the problems of deforestation, pollution and other matters. After seeing this letter, JRD sent an internal note in response. A more detailed response to the letter was later sent to the ex-resident by a senior official of TISCO. JRD's note on the letter was as follows.

A thoughtful and well-meaning letter which deserves to be answered. How come there are no taxis in Jamshedpur? Why have cinemas closed? Spread of television or video? Surely not. Are we doing enough towards re-afforestation on and below Dalma Hill? The thunder of endless truck traffic on the road on which schools are located must be a great nuisance and impediment to teaching. Couldn't some of it be diverted?

This attention to detail is important. Attention to detail and in general aiming for perfection in cases where they do not translate into material or personal benefits are indicative of a sense of ownership based on responsibility and trusteeship. JRD's concern about Jamshedpur and about its taxis and cinemas is part of the sense of responsibility he felt as a trustee of that town. Diverting traffic to help schoolchildren does not benefit the company. And this concern for that town is not JRD's worry alone. For him, everybody should play their role as a trustee in their own limited way.

It is true that there are many other business corporations that are engaged in social welfare. But I think it is reasonable to claim that nowhere and not for so long has one business corporation made social welfare an integral part of its corporate vision. There are many challenges and surely some shortcomings, some aspects of which will be discussed in the concluding chapter. But here it is worthwhile pausing to reflect on how the idea of trusteeship was converted into successful practice. Although none of this reaches the lofty ideals and expectations of Gandhi's aim of trusteeship, we have a framework for possible elaboration of this idea with an emphasis on its practical implementation, an approach that would have suited Gandhi just as well as it suited JRD.

However, to better understand the nature of trusteeship we need to analyse some of the problems associated with its theoretical formulation and practical success. There is no doubt that this seminal idea is extremely important for our society since it offers a non-violent and democratic way of creating a just world, a world which hopefully will be bereft of the senseless poverty that so much pained Gandhi and JRD. In the next chapter, I will briefly discuss some of the problems associated with trusteeship in action, including concepts such as voluntarism, professionalism and social audit.

Notes

1 This chapter was previously published as S. Sarukkai, 'JRD Tata and the Idea of Trusteeship', in M. Jal (ed.), *Zoroastrianism: From Antiquity to the Modern Period*, pp. 307–24, Project of History of Indian Science, Philosophy and Culture (New Delhi: Centre for Studies in Civilizations, 2012), Ministry of Human Resources Development, Government of India.
2 J. R. D. Tata. 'Foreword.' In *Keynote*, edited by S. A. Sabavala and R. M. Lala. Bombay: Tata Press Limited, 1986, pp. xii–xiii.
3 M. K. Gandhi. *Young India*, 20-8-1925, p. 285.
4 Letter to Vasudev, 26 November 1979.
5 It is not obvious that Corporate Social Responsibility (CSR) is a form of trusteeship.
6 M. K. Gandhi. *Trusteeship*. Ahmedabad: Navajivan Publishing House, 1960, p. 5.
7 Ibid., p. 6.
8 *Trusteeship*, op. cit., p. 7.
9 *Trusteeship*, op. cit., p. 22.
10 Ibid., p. 4.
11 *Trusteeship*, op. cit., p. 13.
12 Ibid., p. 10.
13 Ibid., p. 12.
14 Ibid., p. 21.
15 *Trusteeship*, op. cit., p. 5.
16 *Trusteeship*, op. cit., p. 14.
17 *Trusteeship*, op. cit., p. 31.
18 Ibid., p. 32.
19 *Trusteeship*, op. cit., p. 32.
20 Ibid., pp. 39–40.
21 V. Tandon. 'Vinobha and the Theory of Trusteeship.' In *Trusteeship: The Gandhian Alternative*, edited by J. D. Sethi, New Delhi: Gandhi Peace Foundation, 1986.
22 A. Ramamurti. 'Trusteeship in Agriculture.' In *Trusteeship: The Gandhian Alternative*, op. cit.
23 Interview in *Business India*, 27 February 1978.
24 Interview in *Business India*, 27 February 1978.
25 Letter to Shriman Narayan, 20 August 1973.
26 Letter dated 15 November 1985.
27 Letter to Sahni, 16 August 1978.
28 R. M. Lala. *The Heartbeat of a Trust*. New Delhi: Tata McGraw-Hill, 1984.

4

BUSINESS AND SOCIAL WELFARE

Trusteeship is an important formulation for understanding how business and social welfare can be linked. Trusteeship is, of course, not restricted to business but is extendable to all facets of our life. In this chapter, I will discuss some foundational issues related to trusteeship, social justice, social welfare and ways of attaining them.

The very idea of trusteeship is based to some extent on voluntarism. For a long time, voluntarism has been a dominant method of social work and social service. However, there are many questions related to the nature of voluntarism. Why do people volunteer? What are their motivations? What is the relationship between one who volunteers to help somebody and the person receiving that help? What kind of compensation can there be for voluntary work? How much autonomy can a volunteer have? Should a volunteer be accountable for her actions? Many of these questions have become more prominent today as we see a shift from voluntarism to professionalism of social service. Professionalism leads to institutionalisation, thereby removing the dependency on an individual for social work. However, it also dilutes some essential aspects of social service. The first section discusses some of these dilemmas. JRD followed a model of voluntarism as far as his wealth and time were concerned. When it came to his companies, he followed the path of professionalism as the preferred mode for social welfare.

In recent times, it has become important for companies to publicly show social commitment. JRD was way ahead of his times in this too. As part of this new-age capitalism, social audit has become a catchword to indicate a company's broader commitment to society. The Tatas were the first company in India, private or public, to have a social audit of their company, in this case TISCO. In this chapter, I first discuss some basic ideas of social audit and what it might really achieve. Then I summarise TISCO's two social audit reports, one dated 1981 and the other 1991. These reports summarise the various programmes taken up by the company to improve labour welfare, pollution, social welfare and so on. The summary of these reports is intended not only to indicate the range of activities that fall under the domain of social audit but also to understand what is special about the Tata approach to conducting business.

The chapter concludes by arguing that for JRD one of the most important guiding principles was the principle of balance. The idea of balance greatly influenced JRD and was one that moderated his actions. I begin this final section with a discussion on the nature of balance and how this concept has been so influential in almost all spheres of human activities, including science and art. The principle of balance is desirable for one who tries to accommodate differing points of view, rejects the hegemony of one ideology and so on. If we look at JRD's life, we can see that he was always engaging with the possibility of finding the right balance: between the private and public, duty and freedom, autonomy and accountability, business and social commitment. However, all of us live under the shadow of balance in that we try to balance the various constraints in our lives. What was special about JRD's approach was that he chose to find proper balance even when there was no need for him to do so. It is this conscious attempt to create a balance that sets his thought apart. It also allows us to place ideas important to him such as duty, responsibility, freedom and co-existence within a coherent theory of balance.

Social justice: voluntarism or professionalism?

The idea of trusteeship is intrinsically dependent on a prior formulation of justice and, in particular, social justice. Trusteeship demands that we recognise our responsibility not only towards our wealth but also to administering that wealth to improve the lives of others. In this view, humans are essentially social creatures and the basic ethical concept of duty comes from some kind of humanist ethics. Such a view would imply that we are all in a connected web, as discussed in the first chapter.

One of JRD's fundamental concerns was the removal of poverty. He held the view that a high rate of economic growth was an 'essential' condition of social justice. His vision was to ensure that along with growth, there must also be social justice. JRD's approach engages with the notion of voluntarism, namely, voluntarism arising from the individual as well from the company/group/community.

Voluntarism and trusteeship are closely related since taking on the mantle of a trustee should be a voluntary decision. Voluntarism is an important theme in different traditions of service. Some of the most important social movements are based on variations of this theme. Variations include doing something for no monetary benefit or for much less monetary value compared to what is really due for that work. Also, voluntarism is an important ingredient of service in religious and cultural organisations. Medical service has from ancient times been imbued with the spirit of voluntarism.

To volunteer is to do something without expecting anything in return, to act without being expected to do so or without being solicited. In most cases, volunteering implies doing something for others, participating in action which is to the benefit of other people without expecting 'equal' remuneration for that work, working for free and so on. However, why would anybody do something for others for free? An ethical foundation for voluntarism can be found in our social belongingness and our duty to give back to others what we have been fortunate to gain. For example, it is often stated that if one is healthy then it is one's duty to voluntarily help those who are not healthy. Sometimes people volunteer because of this feeling of duty, which may be expressed in various ways such as 'giving back to the less fortunate'. We can immediately see the paradox inherent in voluntarism in these cases. If it is a duty then it is not strictly volunteering. Also, there is a potential problem in that the spirit of voluntarism might dilute the autonomy of individual existence if we are ethically answerable to those not as fortunate as us. It is this tension between doing something because we want to and doing something because we have a duty to doing it that makes voluntarism one of the most difficult models of social service.

What do we volunteer for? Why do we volunteer? And how do we volunteer? Many people volunteer when they find a mechanism that channels their desire for volunteering, such as belonging to religious organisations. The institutionalisation of trusteeship is very much dependent on creating agencies which will enable one to volunteer. Volunteering is essentially related to service, doing something for others, often without being asked or without being expected to do so. The very nature of service is that there is no price expected for doing something for others. Every individual during the course of her professional work does something for another. Every job involves doing something for a client, a consumer and so on. But none of these are called service or volunteerism because there is a compensation for doing something for another. Whether the compensation is just or not is another issue altogether. The central impulse for service comes from this lack of compensation. However, it is often said that service also leads to other kinds of compensation, qualitative ones such as peace and satisfaction. We do not need to extend the scope of compensation in order to fit service within that category. I am interested in non-compensatory activity, what is usually called voluntarism.

We may participate in non-compensatory activity for many reasons. Perhaps it is a source of peace, joy or other such mental states of satisfaction. It could be a religiously driven impulse. It could be socially mediated in the sense that by belonging to a social club that indulges in social service one may participate in some social work just because others also do so. It could also be ethically driven such as buying into the belief that we have a duty to help others who are in a worse situation than us. Psychologically, service may be associated with assuaging guilt, driven by a sense of pity or perhaps even an expression of human empathy. Among all these emotions, I believe the one associated with duty without expecting any kind of payback is the most neutral mode of voluntarism because everything else deals with fragile psychological emotions, including human empathy.

The reason for this view is quite simple and is related to the problem of autonomy. The problem is manifested quite commonly in those who are volunteers. The question is how much 'right' do volunteers have over those they are serving.

By 'right', I mean one that may just be a decision made on another person's behalf. For example, a volunteer helps a community in educating children. Suppose the community does not respond to this service the way the volunteer expects them to – for example, by rejecting some methods used by the volunteer to teach these children. What then should the response of the volunteer be? Ideally, we would say that the volunteer is doing something without expecting anything in return, meaning thereby that she must not expect even acceptance of all that she says. The root of the problem is that the people who receive help also often assert their autonomy and individuality. It is sometimes the case that people who are helped find it demeaning to be helped and see it as an affront to their dignity and self-respect even though the help may be necessary.

There are, unfortunately, essential human problems which consistently arise in the voluntary sector. It has often been noted that sometimes a volunteer expects some kind of positive response or acknowledgement for what she does based on the argument that she has sacrificed a lot in order to 'help'. In these cases, monetary expectation is replaced by psychological ones. The basic point is this: often an individual volunteers because she may feel strongly about a particular issue. Volunteers are driven by different kinds of urges, including those derived from moral positions, empathy towards others and so on. Moreover, volunteering is still something special in a world where indifference is the norm. Thus, an added cost and extra effort is often needed in the act of volunteering.

Once a person makes this extra commitment to volunteering then most often they expect the service-receiver to also show a similar commitment to receiving it. However, this is the cause of an inherent tension in voluntarism. The person who volunteers does it out of her choice but the receiver is not receiving out of voluntarism but out of necessity. This difference is indeed a difficult philosophical problem and underlines once again that the act of the volunteer is not necessary (and that is exactly why we even call them volunteers) whereas the receiver necessarily needs help. This is often manifested in the difference between the volunteers and those they help. Many volunteers who work in rural areas come from urban settings. Volunteers who work in the areas of poverty eradication belong to comparably richer communities. And so on. Thus, it is sometimes felt that voluntarism is possible only for those who have the 'luxury' to help others.

Moreover, there are two other common psychological responses that arise in those who volunteer. Firstly, when the act of voluntarism does not satisfy the urge which originally catalysed the act of volunteering, then disillusionment usually follows. Secondly, when the receiver does not reciprocate in a manner that satisfies the volunteer, then there is again a sense of futility.

However, there have been some qualitative changes in the way voluntarism is understood these days. Nowadays, the language of the giver–receiver binary, one which was quite influential in establishing the discourse of voluntarism, is rarely used. The slogan found today is sharing, partnership and self-help. Also, we need to look at voluntarism in an entirely different way. Many of these problems do not arise when we decouple the psychological motivation for volunteering from an ethical duty to volunteer and serve. Also, when voluntarism is understood as contributing to a community rather than to an individual, it is possible to negate the expectations that arise in interpersonal relationships.

One way to make this happen is to 'professionalise' social service work. To professionalise this kind of work means to place volunteers on a par with others who do different kinds of work. Thus, volunteers become employees; they do the task not only out of empathy or wanting to help others but also because it is their 'job', just like the job of taking care of accounts or working in the factory. This also means that they are paid like other workers and thus they are also accountable. This view also shifts the ethical duty to serve from individuals to organisations. It is this kind of a shift to professional social work that is largely embodied in JRD's approach to this issue.

Institutionalisation is an important mechanism of professionalisation. The fundamental strength of institutionalisation is that programmes are no longer dependent on individual drive and vision but more on structured principles which are not dependent on particular individuals for their growth and sustenance. Social service is a job like any other job. This is equivalent to saying that social service is too important to leave to an individual's sense of duty and morality. Thus, in this case, the agent who is the dominant force behind volunteering is not the individual but an organisation such as an NGO or a company. This shift necessitates moving from individual ethics to group ethics, that is, from understanding the nature of ethical duty of an individual to the ethical duty of organisations. If we look at what JRD did then it is easy to see that his fundamental concern was in establishing a sense of 'group ethics' and not just individual ethics. Professionalisation of service is one step in the creation of an ethics for the group.

So, one can enter the social service sector either driven by an individual impulse alone or as part of a group's vision. The latter is a model of a top-down approach where the group's social sensitivity might trickle down to its members and the former illustrates a bottom-up approach where an individual's vision and drive will have to carry the group and thus is entirely dependent on the individual's proclivities.

In the case of JRD, I think it is easy to see that he took the professional approach to social service long before the NGOs discovered this route. For example, the incorporation of different departments within Tata Steel dealing only with various social service programmes clearly illustrates the professional approach to social service. Not only are these departments evaluated just as any other department in the company but they are also accountable in similar ways. This notion of accountability of social service is one of the most important facets of professionalisation.

In earlier models where one would volunteer to do something, the question of accountability was very tricky. Suppose an individual gave her time and effort in order to spend a few days a week in an education programme. Suppose, as is often the case, there was no remuneration for this work and it was done entirely in the spirit of giving. In this situation, a constant problem that arises is related to the evaluation of the impact of this individual's work. Suppose the community does not find a particular programme or approach useful, or the individual is not able to mobilise the local community or make effective changes. In the earlier view of voluntarism, it was felt that since the individual was doing it all for free, there was really no possibility of making that individual answerable to her actions. However, in the professional model the individual in the field is accountable. What we now need is to delineate the parameters of accountability of the larger organisation which is involved in social service.

Should social work be professionally managed? What does professional management mean in these cases? For example, consider an organisation which is involved in doing voluntary work. How should such an organisation be run? Just because the employees are all volunteers and therefore providing a service to the community (and therefore the country), can the expectations from an organisation not be placed upon them? For example, should such an organisation follow accepted norms of labour relations, salaries, financial audit, and so forth?

These issues can be analysed in great detail but I want to focus on one aspect of professionalisation of these organisations, which is the salary paid to social workers. There are many ethical dilemmas in this issue. If a person is working for the betterment of the extreme poor, is it fair that this person receives an executive's salary, even though he or she may be doing the work of an executive in running a whole organisation? This is the ethical challenge which NGOs have faced and continue to face. The expectation of a high salary and other perks for doing jobs related to poverty eradication and suchlike seems to be ethically challenging given the condition of the people they help. This ethical problem is addressed in different ways; at one extreme some NGOs have executives who are paid very high salaries and at the other there are organisations and some NGOs, including Gandhian organisations, which pay very little. So, should rural development and support to the underprivileged be provided only at the level of voluntarism?

Voluntarism is often associated with an individual's autonomy in the sense that it is the individual's desire, motivation and will to serve that makes them volunteer. However, when one approaches voluntarism in this way, a conflict with expectations is always a possibility. There is another way of understanding voluntarism – not as an autonomous act of the individual but as an act of responsibility. This view relates to the problem of ownership discussed earlier. Just as ownership could be understood as responsibility or authority, so also can we understand voluntarism as reflecting our responsibility or autonomy. It is the former view of responsibility that is more desirable.

JRD's notion of service was not based on an emphasis on personal voluntarism, except in the case of himself. That is, although he placed his wealth in Trusts voluntarily and initiated programmes for social welfare, he did not demand that individuals, such as his employees, volunteer their services for social work. Even when he talked about the need for companies to send their engineers and doctors to help solve problems in surrounding areas, he was referring to the duty of a company and not necessarily the duty of its individual employees.

Thus, when it came to the Tatas' involvement in social development, JRD did not choose the personal voluntary model. Instead, he professionalised this aspect of social service. JRD expected the highest sense of professionalism both in the allocation of money and resources and also in the accountability expected of those who worked in this sector. Thus, the groups in charge of social service programmes at Tata Steel, as described earlier in this chapter, are professionally run. The employees involved in community activity are not expected to work for lower salaries. Thus, voluntarism for the Tatas is primarily voluntarism of the company and not of its employees involved in various programmes. This means that the people involved in social development programmes are doing it as a job, together with its sense of accountability. This is consistent with JRD's demand for accountability in all aspects.

The idea of voluntarism is an extremely important ideal for JRD. The emphasis on corporate voluntarism as against individual voluntarism gave rise to the situation that the employees, by and large, felt that the company was involved in social welfare and thereby did not see any reason to take it upon themselves to be so involved. It also seemed to me that the employees of the various Tata companies were quite unaware of the many social welfare programmes of their companies. If asked, they would say that the Tatas are doing something important for communities but had little idea of the specificities. Furthermore, the involvement of employees at an individual level in social work was somewhat negated by the efficient way in which these programmes were run. Thus, professionalisation might actually have led to an indifference towards social service on the part of their own employees. What is important to remember in the case of voluntarism is that this ideal needs to be nurtured in individuals. There has to be organisations to help individuals channel their interest in voluntary work. Excessive specialisation and professionalisation, I believe, gave the Tata employees an excuse for not living up to the ideal of trusteeship which JRD envisioned for all of us in our own small ways.

However, I believe conscious efforts are now underway to not only educate the employees about what the companies are doing but also to involve them in various programmes. Alongside this is the provision that this involvement would be taken into account in the employee's appraisal and contribution to the company.

To conclude this section: the ideal of voluntarism has been extremely important for the Tatas right from Jamsetji's times. The introduction of labour welfare laws, responsibility to the community and nation, social audit, and so on, were all measures indicating the importance of corporate voluntarism. The professionalisation and institutional mechanisms to sustain the idea of trusteeship are also necessary elements of corporate voluntarism. Choosing the path of corporate voluntarism seemed to be a conscious decision on the part of JRD. The contrast with Gandhian organisations might be useful here. In these organisations, typically great value is ascribed to individual voluntarism, which involves individual sacrifice. There is also the belief that it is difficult to fix a monetary value to social work and hence salary structures are always much lower in these organisations compared to other companies or some NGOs. Some of these organisations are also doing important work and making an appreciable difference. However, they also typically face the problem of excessive dependence on individuals. Once dedicated individual volunteers leave, there are no institutional mechanisms to sustain the social welfare programmes since they are so dependent on an individual's commitment. Thus, the great challenge to trusteeship and our larger responsibilities to society is to find the right balance between individual vision and drive, and mechanisms to make it independent of individuals and personalities.

Social audit

Social audit has become an important mantra for new-age capitalism. However, the motivation for social audit and, in general, social work, has been questioned. The very idea of social audit for profit-making companies has drawn the response that there is some profit motive hidden in these companies taking up social work. This suspicion is reflective of a larger cynicism in modern societies which have tended to define humans in terms of potential use-value. Absolute scepticism is unanswerable, whether it is about social audit or even about some fundamental beliefs we hold. Philosophers have long grappled with finding appropriate responses to absolute scepticism, which is always doubtful of a given explanation. One can always argue that whatever a company does in the name of social service is actually to get material benefit for it – maybe in terms of 'profit' such as peace with the local community, facilitating its expansion in those areas where it is involved in social work, use of resources from these regions or even the more pragmatic reason of getting tax breaks.

For example, an article on social audit begins with this belief that social welfare schemes are not entirely altruistic:

> In fact, more than a dozen companies are drawing up or in the process of implementing a social audit of the impact of their business on stakeholders. The motivation is only partly altruistic; most of these companies have come to the conclusion that businesses that understand their impact on key stakeholders can mould a healthier, more productive corporate culture. In other words, a regular social audit can actually strengthen the bottom line.[1]

The authors of this article note that social audit began in companies in the US in the early 1970s, mostly 'as a response to the nascent consumer and environmental movements.' This was partly based on the reaction of the public and various interest groups who were protesting against pollution and the monopoly practices of some big business corporations. These authors note that even though social audit was conducted in terms of consumer and environmental issues, public disclosure about their activities was not a part of it. Soon the big companies 'abandoned social audits due to difficulty in quantifying social aspects of corporate behavior and a lack of consensus about what to measure.'

From the late 1980s, partly fuelled by the boycott of businesses that were associated with the racist South African government, new demands were placed on businesses to follow not only environmental audit but also show sensitivity to social issues. In particular, the belief that businesses that associated with inhuman regimes (and thus indirectly supported their existence) should be boycotted implied that these businesses paid a price for their social indifference. In recent times, we have seen examples of boycott of companies which employ child labour, those which have indulged in corruption, and so on. All these demands are a reflection of the fact that consumers, or at least some of them, do not accept the view that business products can be dissociated from the wider value system of the business that produces it. In an important sense, this demand is nothing more than the position that the ends are not as important as the means to those ends. The means towards production would therefore include issues such as the environment, impact on society, structures that support racism, child labour or labour exploitation, and these issues of production are not to be dissociated from the product.

Therefore, social audit comes closest to taking seriously Gandhi's emphasis on the means over the end. Gandhi propounded a simple binary structure of values that were important to him such as need–want and ends–means. What social audit is doing is bringing the means of production (and sales, distribution etc.) into the ethical domain of the means and thereby negating the emphasis on just the value of the end product.

In the mid-1990s, there were various attempts to find appropriate measures of social audit. However, as the authors of the above article note, a critical weakness in many of these approaches was 'the lack of emphasis on corporate governance and control systems designed to provide assurance that high-minded codes of conduct serve more than just a public relations function.' They also list the different types of social audit that have been tried over the last decade. These include creating a social performance index, independent social assessments, stakeholder surveys, benchmarking by objectives and disclosure reports where evaluation is based on the disclosure of critical information that concerns the many types of stakeholders. Finally, they conclude by suggesting that:

> [A] successful social audit requires a company to demonstrate its commitment to publicly disclose information about company operations and its responsiveness to solve problems uncovered by the audit. There are also indications that management emphasis of ethical qualities as an important part of a company's governance and control structure is strongly and positively associated with measures of corporate performance in both financial and non-financial dimensions. Most critically, a social and ethical evaluation should appraise the effectiveness of control mechanisms, how the company monitors its ethical compliance and whether an independent corporate board exercises ethical oversight.[2]

Thus, social audit manifests two characteristics which we tend to ignore. One is that the means towards achieving something are as important as the end and the other is that we cannot forget the fact that we are always part of a larger organic whole. Both these characteristics are constantly in tension with the way we understand business today, especially in the public imagination. Also, one of the central influences of modern civilisation is the importance ascribed to the autonomy of the individual. This idea, as discussed in various contexts earlier in this book, is one of the central pillars of capitalism. Translated into business concerns, this is nothing more than the statement that businesses should be allowed to flourish with minimum intervention from larger power entities such as the State or even the constraints of social ethics.

However, it is worth asking why social audit should be applicable mainly to the business domain. Why is it not applied to government concerns in the service sector or to educational institutions, for example? This question is important as it illustrates a particular view about business that is quite popularly enshrined as a suspicion about any business motive other than profit. This suspicion towards business is also shared in the suspicion about voluntary action and a scepticism that helping others is tinged with the possibility that one is only helping oneself in helping others.

But it is also true that being human is always an attempt to transcend the limitations of all that is human. Scientific inventions illustrate the attempts to transcend the physical limitations of our senses and body. Ethics in this sense shares a common concern with science and other human activities, including art, which all constantly attempt to redefine the boundaries of human action and thought. Ethics, in formulating the possibility of engaging in ethical acts or what are seen as ethical acts in a given community at a particular time, is also attempting to articulate how we can transcend so-called human proclivities and tendencies. Thus, it is no surprise that ethics deals with the issues of 'what ought to be', 'how we ought to behave' etc. In doing so, ethics tacitly accepts that our actions are based on the image we have of ourselves at the moment of action. And thus, to change our actions it would be useful to change the image. For example, suppose we thought that a particular act of chivalry towards a woman is part of the culture of masculinity, then we would tend to act that way without realising that this act might go against the interests of the particular individual. This action is actually well intentioned since it is dictated by the image we hold about ourselves. So, changing the image in this sense changes the kinds of acts that we would voluntarily perform.

It is this change in image – the image of the businessman and the business community in general – that JRD was so concerned about. His notion of trusteeship and his emphasis on the social, ethical and national responsibility of business corporations and concerns are ways by which he tried to infuse new images of business, images that would dictate how these businesses would behave. Social and ethical responsibilities are components of this image of business which JRD continued to articulate throughout his life.

It is no wonder then that social audit in India was first taken up by a Tata company, namely, TISCO. It was the first company, private or public, to undertake social audit. Two social audit reports are available, dated 1981 and 1991. I will summarise these reports in order to explain the social commitment of a business group and the lessons that we can learn about trusteeship and social welfare in general.

A committee consisting of Mr Justice S. P. Kotval as the Chairman and Profs Rajni Kothari and P. G. Mavalankar as Members was formed 'to go into the question whether and to what extent the Company had fulfilled its obligations under the broad head of social and moral responsibilities under Article 3A of its Articles of Association.'[3] The social and moral responsibilities mentioned above are responsibilities in five different spheres: towards the consumers, employees, shareholders, society and the local community.

The social audit reports of 1981 and 1991 list the various expenditures incurred by the company in providing various municipal activities in Jamshedpur. For example, the first report mentions that the cost of housing for its employees (and partially for non-employees) including schools and hospitals was over nine crores. The supply of filtered water to the city involved heavy expenditure. An underground sewerage and drainage system was run at a deficit of many lakhs every year. The Jubilee park, a popular place for the residents of the city, was built at a cost of 21 lakhs and maintained at appreciable expenditure. This park is a public facility. The first report also mentions the expenditure on health and medical services, including the large hospital run by TISCO.

The reports also discuss the working conditions in both the factories and the mines and analysed the problem of pollution, which was found to be appreciable in the working environment. Meetings with labour leaders were summarised and the generally good relationship between the labour and management was noted. A mechanism that contributed to this positive relationship was the availability of the Managing Director to answer any questions and clarifications from the workers, at a particular time every week. There was also a tradition whereby the MD personally replied to any letter from a worker, independent of the rank of the employee, a practice that seemed to have helped communication between employees and management. An effective grievance redressal system was in place for a long time. The report also notes that there had been no strike in Jamshedpur (on grounds of industrial dispute) for over fifty years.

Similarly, the response to consumers was also found to be satisfactory. As far as the shareholders were concerned, the report mentioned that some shareholders were unhappy about the company's policy of better wages and other benefits to the labour. This observation is important as it points to the potential conflict of interest between the shareholders and the vision of the company. It illustrates a potential conflict between the expectations of shareholders, which might be entirely economic, as against the broader vision of social accountability by the company. This is a problem manifested in almost every organisation which works for social upliftment. The problem is that the vision of an individual will not necessarily be shared by those who are the person's 'shareholders', the ones who matter to that individual. For example, the conflict between a social worker, who sacrifices appreciable economic benefits while working for the betterment of a community, and her immediate family who may not share her commitment is one that is unfortunately all too common.

It has often been remarked that one of the great drawbacks of voluntarism is the price expected by an individual of his or her immediate family. The price one pays in various ways with respect to the family is well known and Gandhi's example in this regard has been well documented. This is similar to the conflict that arises when the values of the stakeholders are in opposition to those of the management. For example, if the children of a rich man feel that their father is squandering his money on social welfare then there is a conflict of interest. In the context of trusteeship, this problem was recognised as a fundamental one, which made Gandhi insist that the heirs of a trustee should not necessarily be family members. The concept of trusteeship would therefore necessitate that the shareholders can only be trustees if they accept their company's role as a trustee of their wealth. It is worthwhile noting that even with these potential problems, JRD not only insisted on the commitment to social welfare but also to increasing the resources and efficiency of such programmes. But in doing so, the shareholders were also kept satisfied because of the financial success of these companies.

The 1981 report notes that community development and social welfare programmes had been an integral part of the company for a long time. By the time of the first report, there was a separate department in charge of these affairs, which supported many activities such as training in craft making, classes for children and special programmes for Adivasis. There was also a new rural development programme set up to help agriculture and crop extension in many surrounding villages. There was a plan for supporting poultry farming and some village industries. The 1981 report notes that as part of agriculture support, the company had embarked on building three dams. It had supplied irrigation and pump sets including pipes for distributing water. This material help was augmented by an expert trained in agriculture who visited the villages and was available for consultation with the farmers. Innovative programmes in poultry farming were envisioned and began at this time. The company had also started a 'Village Industries Centre' where about 100 villagers would be trained in the manufacture of various small items such as soap, products which had a big market in the local area itself. It was projected that this programme could in itself generate about 2000 jobs.

Finally, the report concludes by cataloguing various other activities supported by the company at a national level, such as working towards smallpox eradication in the Chottanagpur Division, flood relief for various parts of Bihar, and cyclone relief work in Orissa and Andhra Pradesh. The report commends the extraordinary voluntary commitment of the company to social welfare while also making a few suggestions for streamlining some aspects of it. The total expenditure on social welfare schemes was about Rs 10 crores per year. The cost of this was borne by the company. The report underlines the fact that this cost was not passed on to the consumers or the shareholders.

The second social audit report was prepared ten years later in 1991. The committee consisted of Mr Justice D. N. Mehta (Retd) as the Chairman and Profs P. G. Mavalankar and Sachchidananda as Members. Like the first report, this too stays clear of a larger theoretical framework of what social audit is or could be. In particular, it does not engage with any use of quantitative measures of social audit. Many of the points discussed in the earlier report also find a place here. This report also analyses the policies and impact of programmes to help the employees, consumers, shareholders and the larger community. In the case of management of the town, it notes that the total cost of doing so worked out at Rs 46.62 crores, out of which the company spent Rs 38.79 crores. New construction works in the town included additions to the hospitals, college and hostels, a zoo in the Jubilee park, maintaining eleven public markets in the town and the supply of pure drinking water.

The second report also discusses the progress made on the pollution front. It points out that the first social audit report had passed certain strictures in this regard. Five years after the first report, a new department called the Environmental Management Division was founded. Although impressive progress had been made in controlling pollution, especially in the mines, the committee concludes that more should be done, particularly in the Steel Works.

The report on social welfare activities in this report was broken up into two separate chapters. The Community Development and Social Welfare Department continued many of its activities in health and medical welfare, activities for children and women, and education activities, with the main thrust being family planning and health care programmes. The other chapter focuses on the Tata Steel Rural Development Society, a scheme started in 1979 at the initiative of JRD. This group works with villages not only around Jamshedpur but also in those surrounding West Bokaro, Noamundi and other places. The report notes that in the ten years leading to the second social audit report, the company had spent a sum of Rs 10 crores on these projects. One of the innovative schemes initiated by this Society was the pani panchayat, which transformed the distribution and management of water supply.

One of the categories highlighted in this report, in contrast to the previous one, was the support given to sports by the Tatas. In TISCO alone, there was a separate Sport and Welfare Department with an annual budget of Rs 87.50 lakhs. There is a long tradition of support to various sporting activities by the Tatas. Dorabji Tata was the first chairman of the Indian Olympic Association and over the years the company had sponsored many Olympians. It had also supported adventure sports such as mountaineering. In 1982, the company started the Tata Steel Sports Foundation. Now there are two stadiums, a hostel, gymnasium and various other support facilities to train young sportsmen and women in various sporting disciplines. We have already noted the support given to archery and football. In keeping with the spirit of adventure, one that was an essential component of JRD's view of life, the Tatas have also founded a Tata Steel Adventure Club. It is no surprise that Jamshedpur is called the sports city of India.

The second report ends with some suggestions, pointing out that there was a 'total lack of awareness among the shareholders and the consumers' regarding the various facets of welfare schemes and other non-business matters of the company. Even the employees of the company had only a 'foggy idea of the social obligation rendered by the Company to the community at large.' Various other suggestions were largely to do with improving the general economic and material welfare of the employees, implementing greater pollution control measures and so on. The report concluded by noting that the 'social conscience' of the company still remained strong, and that the relation with labour, shareholders and the surrounding community had been maintained and strengthened.

There is no doubt that these two reports are useful, at least as a catalogue of the various activities outside the domain of pure business. However, the reports do not elaborate on any of the themes related to social audit. They also do not evaluate the impact of many of these social welfare programmes. Moreover, unless there is a deeper analysis of why and how business concerns should do the job of social service, these facts would only be indicative of an attempt and not of a well-thought-out vision. But when taken in conjunction with JRD's philosophy and the various themes which we have already discussed, we can see that JRD's approach, particularly that of trusteeship which is the catalysis for many of these activities, is not only indicative of careful reflection on the nature of social service but also a practical model that can be analysed and built upon.

Social responsibilities according to JRD: a fine balance

There are two important aspects of JRD's vision on social responsibility. One is the relationship between the local community and a company. As JRD explained, 'every Company has a special continuing responsibility towards the people of the area in which it is located and in which its employees and their families live.'[4] There are many ways by which a company can have a relationship with the local community. For JRD, as much as programmes were important, it was also necessary for the personnel of the company to be available to share their expertise and resources with the surrounding community. So, he suggested that 'the most significant contribution organised industry can make is by identifying itself with the life and problems of the people of the community to which it belongs and by applying its resources, skills and talents, to the extent that it can reasonably spare them to serve and help them.'[5]

Social responsibility can only be a secondary aspect of a company's function. However, it is a *necessary* part of a company's activities. It is this insight that is reflected consistently in JRD. There is one philosophical theme that is useful to invoke in this context. It is a theme which, I believe, was essential to JRD's understanding of his world. This is the idea of balance.

The idea of balance is quite important in many human activities, whether it is business, arts or science. Balance is often used synonymously with various other terms such as harmony, simplicity, beauty and symmetry. Balance is one of the important principles at the foundation of our aesthetic experience, whether it is visual, auditory or taste. A balance of tastes is an essential component of a good dish. The idea of balance is important for many reasons. It has not only an aesthetic value but also an ethical one. As a principle it is of great importance to science, as manifested in the centrality of the idea of symmetry in science. So, ranging from food to art to science, the idea of balance has a special value.

In visual perception, we often respond favourably to the balance of various elements in a visual picture. In music, aesthetically pleasing music often exhibits a balance of notes and harmonies. In common use of language, 'being off-balance' implies a sense of instability and the possibility of collapse. Common idioms express this importance of balance. For example, the saying 'All work and no play makes Jack a dull boy' indicates the importance of balancing work and play. In the context of the intellectual tradition, the synthesis of mind and body is often seen to be important. Focusing on one at the expense of the other is not desirable – not desirable for a wholesome sense of living. In psychological terms, we often speak of mental balance, which is the capacity to maintain equilibrium in our mental thoughts.

Even conceptually, we find that the idea of balance is extremely important in that it brings together different contrary themes. For example, science is possible only by bringing together theoretical reflection and experimental observation. In principle, theory and experiments are like two contrary activities but the discipline of science is possible because it is able to bring these together and find the right balance in their togetherness. Unlike 'pure' thought which has no input from experience, science believes that thought has to be complemented with experience, primarily observations. In fact, the strength of science comes from this balance between theory and experiment and also between science (theoretical) and technology (practical).

An insight into JRD can be obtained through analysing his attempts to articulate the sense of balance in his vision of the world, including the business world. If we consider those ideas that were essential to JRD, we find that all or most of them bring together divergent concepts in a way that illustrates a sense of balance. For example, his thoughts on a mixed economy bring together the notions of private and public as also the notions of private and government. In his approach to conducting business, we can see his attempts to strike a balance between autonomy and accountability. In the case of social welfare along the lines of trusteeship, we can clearly see the balance that is being sought between profit and service, between voluntarism and professionalism. In the description of the individual, we see the conflict between being an individual and being a social being. Striking a balance between duty and freedom was another important theme for JRD.

I think it is clear, as these examples illustrate, that for JRD one of the most important principles that regulated his action was that of the principle of balance. What is special about this idea of balance? In our lives, we are constantly balancing between various constraints. Having a balanced view is also indicative of living harmoniously with problems and constraints. Whenever there are constraints in anything we do, as often there are, we make do, manage to the best of our abilities. In so doing, we are perpetually finding a balanced way to act.

However, JRD's emphasis on balance is not the balance that we are forced into when we function under constraints. JRD was emphasising the balance that we *create by choice* and not the balance that arises because of a need. Although he doesn't explicitly say so, I believe that, for him, to be in a state of balance was one of the most important ethical principles – one that goes beyond following specific ethical principles. Moreover, the state of balance had to be reached by choice and not through circumstances. Thus, JRD's constant engagement with various programmes and policies for social and labour welfare, for example, can be understood as attempts to find what in his mind was the proper balance. As mentioned earlier, all these attempts were done of his own volition and not because of needs such as pleasing his workers or getting a tax break.

Why should a principle of balance be so important to JRD? What is it in the idea of balance that so best describes his actions? Basically, the idea of balance is the doctrine that captures a variety of themes: it speaks against excess of any kind, of privileging one thing entirely over another and points to the necessity of incorporating more than one view in a coherent manner. Equivalently, the doctrine of balance would claim that one idea, one principle, one approach should not dominate over other possible ones that may be contrary or even contradictory to it. There is no hegemony of a single, monolithic entity that is allowed within a philosophy of balance. This, therefore, implies that even ethical principles cannot dictate and dominate a particular action because ethics too needs to be moderated according to the principle of balance. Being in balance is to be in equilibrium. Ethical principles cannot be independent of contexts. This is one rule of ethics that is increasingly finding acceptance in mainstream discourse. We have seen examples of such ethical approaches, most notably in ethical debates in Indian philosophy. What we ought to do in a particular context is dictated not by a universal principle, although such a principle might suggest ways of action, but more by principles that are sensitive to the given situation and context. Bringing ethical principles into business practices actually also helps to bring ethical considerations into contemporary life as much as it tightens business into following more desirable practices.

Thus, adhering to a principle of balance means that every action we take has to be moderated by a balance of various interests and forces. In any action, one cannot be purely selfish, cannot expect only material profit and so on. We have seen right from the first chapter the various ways by which ideas such as profit, autonomy, accountability, private and public were all made answerable to the principle of balance. The expansion of the meanings of these ideas is a consequence of finding meanings that capture a sense of balance. Striking a balance means finding ways to accommodate different views. One of the important ways to strike a balance, to maintain equanimity, is by understanding the idea of co-existence. It is no accident that for JRD both democracy and co-existence were very important ideas.

We can best understand JRD's philosophy of action through the filter of the principle of balance. We can see it in his support for the mixed economy, an economy in which public and private sectors function together. In September

1953, in the Chairman's Statement of TISCO, JRD clarified the nature of a mixed economy in terms of a 'balance of forces, with free enterprise operating as one of the autonomous forces pulling its weight alongside State enterprises, trade unions and other elements in society.'[6] Furthermore, JRD accepted that he was not demanding a totally free-market economy and added that the 'interests of the nation as a whole must prevail over the interests of the few.'[7] One of the important consequences of a balance thus established will be in helping to 'instil in the private sector the sense of trusteeship advocated by Mahatma Gandhi and would put squarely upon it [private sector] the responsibility for placing national above sectional and personal interests.'[8] For those who would claim that JRD's statements might not mean much, they have to realise that these statements were not only public statements but were also backed by action, both in his response to the government by working for it as the Chairman of Air-India and also to his fellow entrepreneurs whom he continuously extolled to follow a more balanced approach. I believe that what gave clarity and coherence to JRD's actions was this idea of balance.

It is clear that the establishment of a 'fine balance' is central to the debate between the public and private, especially for JRD. He explained that the essence of a mixed economy is that while the exact share of State and private enterprise in 'ownership and management of economic assets' may differ from country to country, 'they should invariably co-exist.'[9] This idea of the *co-existence* of the State and private enterprise is absolutely central to JRD's thought. The idea of balance is captured in that of co-existence: whether it is co-existence of the State and private enterprise, industry and the surrounding community, private freedom and public responsibility, management and labour, etc.

For JRD, democracy was essential to co-existence. Democracy and co-existence indicate methods that allow us to reach a balance. Even in the case of social welfare, especially of the tribal communities, the word that JRD preferred was co-existence and not words such as assimilation. This he did long before co-existence became politically correct.

None of this implies that JRD always knew the best way to approach a problem or find the best solution. I do not think that such an expectation is applicable to any of us, however farsighted and wise the individual may be. JRD's approach was a pragmatic one but he did not use the excuse of pragmatism to do what he wanted. He accepted the importance of adhering to certain ethical rules, even though it is clear that he would have accepted their context dependence. In JRD's approach to living a life of balance, we can also see the pitfalls of balance. One is the problem of excessive consensus, a move that might impede decision-making. JRD acknowledged in an interview that he had been criticised for being 'too much of a consensus man.'[10] In the final analysis, living a life moderated by the principle of balance is also a humanist approach to living, one that acknowledges that we never live our lives as an individual but are part of a vibrant human web.

Notes

1 C. C. Verschoor and J. H. Entine. 'Social Auditing: Oxymoron or Wave of the Future?' Available at www.jonentine.com.
2 Ibid.
3 Social Audit Report, 1981, p. 1.
4 Quoted in the Annual Report 2002–03 of the Tribal Cultural Society.
5 Ibid.
6 J. R. D. Tata. *Keynote*. Edited by S. A. Sabavala and R. M. Lala. Bombay: Tata Press Limited, 1986, p. 46.
7 Ibid., p. 47.
8 Ibid., p. 47.
9 Ibid., p. 53.
10 R. M. Lala. *The Joy of Achievement: Conversations with J.R.D. Tata.* New Delhi: Viking, 1995, p. 72.

5

PRIVATE AND THE PUBLIC

JRD lived during a time that saw, among other momentous events, the Revolution in Russia, two World Wars, the growth of industries in America after a terrible period of depression, the dawn of Independence in India, a galaxy of Indian leaders who established high ethical standards of public conduct, and soon after Independence a government that believed in socialism. In many ways, he was a man who was perpetually caught in between: between France and India in his early years, between an adventurous spirit and his responsibility as an heir to a business tradition, drawn by the political strength of people like Gandhi and Nehru but uncomfortable with their economic views, a pioneer in private industries but a proponent of public, social welfare and so on. Perhaps reflective of his times and of his own position of being in between two ends, his own actions and writings indicate some powerful binaries at work, such as private/public, autonomy/accountability, power/responsibility and freedom/duty. To understand JRD's philosophical insights it is necessary to engage with this intermediary position in which he often found himself. Finding himself constantly negotiating between extremes, JRD also realised the importance of the idea of balance, an idea which, as we saw earlier, profoundly influenced his professional life.

This chapter begins with a discussion of the notions of private and public. JRD was a doyen of private enterprise but was also a representative of the government in his capacity as the Chairman of Air-India. He was the Chairman of the Tata group during a period when there were more obstacles to growth than support. He was a passionate believer in the spirit that defined private enterprise but at the same time wanted it voluntarily tempered with social responsibility. The understanding of our society through the categories of private and public means that inordinate importance is given to these two categories as if they are not only independent of each other but also exclusive of one another. This distinction is itself debatable.

It is reasonable to believe that JRD was uncomfortable with the strict demarcation of the conceptual ideas of the private and public. A related set of themes that are necessary for an understanding of public and private is that of autonomy and accountability. What JRD tried to do was to find ways to explore the interconnectedness of these ideas. Autonomy is often related to the notion of private and accountability to that of public. JRD turned this on its head and demanded that autonomy should be expected of the public and accountability of the private. This is one of the most influential and challenging formulations both for the private and public sectors.

The last set of themes that I discuss in this chapter is that of power and control. Again, these ideas are very closely related to that of the public and private as well as autonomy and accountability. For JRD, being responsible was one of the defining characteristics of an individual. The challenge to responsibility comes when one has power. It is during this moment that we have to be most responsible because it is in the nature of power that one might cease to be responsible. JRD consistently argued that it was extremely important that just as the private individual needed to inculcate responsibility so also should private industries act with greater responsibility not just with regard to their company and needs but with respect to the larger society to which they belong.

The ideas of private and public

We make sense of the world around us by creating various categories, and the categories we create may depend on many social and cultural factors. For example, in many Indian languages, the category of uncle is further refined into words such as 'father's younger brother', 'father's older brother' and so on. These categories describe the way the users of these languages relate to their uncles. Similarly, our understanding of the natural and social world depends on the categories we have to describe them. Depending on our interests we might construct different categories. For example, it is well known that the Eskimos have more than twenty words to describe various aspects of snow. Each of these words describes some special characteristics of snow, reflecting the different types and uses of snow as they see it.

Similarly, 'private' and 'public' are two categories that we use to make sense of the social world in a particular way. These two categories that are used to describe the society around us have become so commonplace that we tend to think that there is something natural about the dichotomy between the private and the public. But this is not so. The ideas of private and public are categories which we use to order our society in a *particular* way. This implies that these categories are not natural or necessary in that we could have made sense of the world without looking at it through the filter of these categories or without the meanings we attach to these categories now.

Our understanding of the world depends to some extent on the meaning of this binary of the private and public. It is not that we have always and in all cultures described ourselves through this binary. Smaller cultures and tribal communities may have a very different formulation of these ideas, if they are used in any such sense at all.

It has been suggested that the establishment of this binary has strong roots in the Western Enlightenment tradition, one that gave rise to the culture of modernity as we understand it now. An important characteristic of modernity was the shift to the autonomy of the individual, to privileging human reason and placing human capacity at the forefront of change and growth. The beliefs that an individual must be measured in terms of her worth, that an individual is indeed a monadic entity wholly autonomous and answerable only to herself, that an individual has the right to demand and expect of herself what she wants to do and how she wants to do it, have all contributed to the sustenance of capitalism as something that privileges individual capacity and the will to succeed. The placement of the autonomous individual at the centre of the world is a great revolution which has changed the way we understand the ideas of private and public.

The impact of this move towards individual autonomy as against the autonomy of the family, community, nation or God has made possible not only revolutions in economic, scientific and artistic spheres but also in politics, as best exemplified by the democratic ideal. This ideal is not only based on the belief that every vote of an adult citizen should count but also that every adult has a right to exercise this vote. Along with the emphasis on individual human autonomy, the idea of private and public begins to acquire greater meaning and importance. The idea of private can and does exist even without a clear centring of the individual (for example, as in the case of a family and society to represent private and public, respectively). The emphasis on individual and individual autonomy carries forward the idea of private to a different dimension.

Thus, over the last three to four centuries the binary of private and public has gathered different kinds of meanings. Now it is one of the defining binaries of modern cultures. In today's societies, the importance of privacy, an idea essentially related to that of the private, is manifested in different spheres of human activity. Even in the case of residence, privacy has become an important category. A common example illustrates this well. It has been pointed out that in earlier times Indian homes were not exclusively described through the category of bedrooms. Presumably a description of Indian homes in these times might not have referred to them as two- or three-bedroom houses. In contrast, the emphasis on bedrooms, which are in their own way essentially associated with privacy, has become the standard description of homes in modern India.

The issue of the private in the public arena is one of the most contentious issues of modern times and is most strikingly illustrated in the United States. Constitutional fights over invasion of privacy have defined American society over the years. There is a two-sidedness to this cultural space of the individual so well illustrated and caricatured by the American experience: the absolute right to privacy and rights of the individual and *at the same time* the responsibility of the government to be transparent. Thus, while individuals will have an inaccessible core of privacy, the government must in principle allow access to the information it has, except in certain cases related to such matters as national security.

In any given binary like light and dark, man and woman or private and public, it is often the case that one term of the binary is privileged and is prior to its 'opposite', a point made in a philosophical context by the French philosopher, Derrida. In the case of private and public, we seem to have a similar situation in that, following the period of Enlightenment, the idea of the private is privileged. What this means is that we can define what it means to be private without drawing upon and contrasting with the idea of the public. Thus, in this particular culture, private is defined in terms of the autonomous individual and the public therefore becomes that which is not the private. The many strictures placed on the public's 'right' over the individual indicates the priority of the private/individual over the public, at least in certain domains.

However, the public is nothing more than a collection of individuals, although a collection of individuals does not necessarily become a public entity. What happens when individuals join together to form the public? What element of the individual is lost in this coming together? And what is strengthened? I want to look at only one of the many factors that create the public entity from private individuals. This is the element of responsibility. One of the most important elements in the formation of a group is the voluntary abdication of one's autonomy. The first important lesson we learn in groupings is that there will always be an occasion where we have to give up our own inclinations and desires. Thus, the very action of bringing individuals together also negates one important aspect of individual autonomy.

The real trick lies in negotiating between an individual's autonomy and collective decisions. JRD's way of dealing with people illustrates the many problems in the relation between an individual and the group to which she belongs. It has been said that JRD avoided taking certain decisions and letting the larger consensus prevail. In this context, it is interesting to see what he had to say.

> I am disinclined to take hard decisions because they would create unpleasantness. But I personally feel, though I may be wrong, that keeping a certain constancy in the way people regard you, in the way you relate to people will result in a good net result over the long term. You know, it is like a family. You can't take strong, hard decisions throughout, fire so and so, get rid of so and so, back up one side of the family rather than another. I know that all my colleagues have their own views and on many views of theirs I don't agree and they don't agree perhaps with mine. But, generally, we have always come to feel that we are doing the best that we can and that we are sincere and that we mean to do the right thing.[1]

He went on to add:

> If I have any merit, it is getting on with individuals according to their ways and characteristics. At times it involves suppressing yourself. It is painful but necessary... To be a leader you have got to lead human beings with affection.

JRD was thus aware of the fundamental tension between individual autonomy and group membership, as well expressed in his statement that one has to suppress oneself, an act which is 'painful and necessary'. For a culture that privileges human individuality, this conflict leads to profound problems, which are not just between individuals in a group but are also manifested in the relation between the private and the public sectors.

Before we proceed further, a clarification on my use of individual/private. The association of the idea of private with the individual has also been influential in the meaning of private as in private companies. In the case of the individual, the individual is contrasted to that of a larger community, thus constituting the private–public binary. From the viewpoint of the individual and his or her autonomy, any group is part of the public in that they are not privy to a domain of knowledge and experience that is for the individual alone. In this case, the correct binary is the personal–social. The meanings of personal and its opposition to social are meanings that are in most cases specific to an individual. Now, it is often possible to talk of a group as 'private', as in private companies, Trusts or organisations owned by a group of individuals. How is it that this collection of individuals retains a notion of the 'private'? Or, in other words, what exactly is 'private' about a private company? One answer to this question is described below but at this point in the discussion I merely want to point out that the private–public binary borrows some essential themes from the personal–social binary. Therefore, what I say about the individual can with little reflection be transferred to the 'private'.

JRD's way of dealing with the tension between individual autonomy and group membership illustrates a theme common to his views on various other aspects such as profit, trusteeship and so on. This is the theme of responsibility. A group can effectively function only when an individual decides to place the interest of the group above that of the individual. An individual has to *decide* consciously to sacrifice his or her interests if the group is to survive. In other words, being responsible is also an autonomous act of the individual. Thus, responsibility actually retains the spirit of the human individual (because it is the individual who *decides* to be responsible) even as it allows the possibility of different individuals coming together to form a group.

Responsibility is not only a one-way movement from the individual to the group. The group also has a responsibility to the individual. Primarily, this responsibility lies in acknowledging that an individual through conscious choice decides to support the group even at the expense of the individual's opinions and beliefs. Thus, ideally, the individual's role in a group is to be responsible even at the expense of one's personal interests while the responsibility of the group towards the individual is to leave the matter of responsibility on the individual and not enforce it as a group decision.

It is this sense of responsibility that JRD demanded not only of himself but of other public entities, including the government. However, the nature of responsibility is different in the case of individuals when compared to the group. In the case of an individual, to be responsible is a decision made by the person whereas responsibility in a group is part of the institutionalisation process. Given the nature of the group and the ever-persistent possibility of conflict with the individual, a group's responsibility is best defined through institutional mechanisms. Therefore, it is not a surprise that we find in JRD (and the Tatas in general) an institutionalisation of group responsibility.

It is reasonable to claim that the nature of responsibility became one of JRD's most important concerns, both in understanding the nature of his business as well as its role in a larger society. Focusing on responsibility with the characteristics described above has many consequences. First of all, the idea of responsibility must inform both private and public behaviour and action. Explicitly understanding responsibility as that which binds individuals into a group makes it difficult to have ethical anarchy. Furthermore, there is greater responsibility the more you speak for others; thus, belonging to a group increases that sense of responsibility. Also, the way we represent ourselves as belonging to the domain of 'private' and others as belonging to that of 'public' undergoes important changes when we understand that all of us function under the constraint of responsibility. The responsibility that we hold makes us distinguish between what we speak in private and in public. For example, even when JRD was at the height of disagreement with the government over various issues, he always refrained from criticising the government when outside the country. This is one kind of responsibility that he felt was important to him.

For JRD, the culture of the private individual influenced that individual's image as part of a public entity. The culture of the private is our individual culture drawn from factors such as traditions, membership, identity and status. Just as the culture of the individual is shaped in many ways and is dependent on factors right from birth, JRD was concerned about creating a culture of the public. His approach to this was well represented in his deeds – the sense of social responsibility which he thought was important to any business concern, the idea of trusteeship which informed his approach towards all the stakeholders, bringing individual aesthetics to the public domain, such as in the urban planning of Jamshedpur, to name one example.

However, there are quite a few problems in categorising the exact nature of the private and public. First of all, the nature of the public seems to be quite amorphous. Although we can agree that the notion of the public is already present in any grouping of individuals, it is not necessarily the case that a group constitutes a public. To be public also means access to that group or the activities of the group by the larger community of people who do *not* belong to that group. *Secrecy* and *inaccessibility* in some sense is an important indicator of the nature of the private. (We can see the relation between private and personal in this example of secrecy and inaccessibility since to be an individual is to have an inaccessible subjective core.) So, we may have a group, however big or small it may be, which is exclusive and whose workings are not available for public discussion and for public information, thus indicating their 'private' nature. On the other hand, the very idea of 'public' negates the attempt to secrecy, and the responsibility of the public enterprise is to make sure its workings are not only transparent but also accountable to a larger public, even to those who do not have direct links with the enterprise. In other words, the stakeholders of a public organisation are the public themselves. For example, the right to information movement pioneered in some places in India over the last few years (for example, by the Mazdoor Kisan Shakti Sangathan) illustrates the perennial tension between secrecy, privacy, the private sector and the right to information demanded from the government, which, all said and done, is one mammoth public-sector enterprise!

There is also a problem about who constitutes the public. Is it the immediate community, districts, states or the central government? The idea of the public is mediated in different ways in different arenas such as politics, culture and business. The public in a democratic system is a quite different entity from the public who inhabit a public space. Furthermore, in the context of accountability, it is not clear to whom one should be accountable in the domain of the public. If there are representatives within the public who stand for it, like elected members of the Parliament, then how are they accountable to the system? Democracy seemingly introduces a measure of accountability – but it doesn't work in the way that we hope it should. JRD consistently argued that economic totalitarianism (practised, in his view, by a democratically elected government) was as bad as political totalitarianism.

On the other hand, there is also something problematic with the notion of private, at least the notion which many hold. The problem arises because fundamentally we are social beings and social citizens. We are born into a social world and what we do, what we have, our hopes, dreams etc. are all made possible by the public sphere around us. This public world limits our actions as much as it makes possible our initiatives. Our particular social standing in a large sense decides the choices that we have. Since we are never really an individual in the sense of having pure individual autonomy, we are always part of a system, which may be a composite of various factors such as class, caste, religion and tradition.[2] The often-quoted statement that we always stand on the shoulders of others is apt in many ways. If this is so, if we are indebted to various other factors including the larger society, then in what sense can we demand the autonomy due to an individual?

As an individual we know that we have various duties to perform. Every individual accepts his or her duty to their family, job and so on. The point is that as individuals we feel responsible for something around us, in most cases at least for our immediate families. Thus, the individual's autonomy is always being compromised by various other factors. In all these duties, what is the duty of the individual to the public? Or to a larger public sphere, something which goes beyond immediate family or community? This is the fundamental question that is posed to the distinction we make when we invoke the idea of private and the public. This is a question that acknowledges that in the private individual there is a shared space of the public. Although JRD does not reflect on the idea of private and public along these lines, it is clear that elements of this analysis are scattered in his collection of letters, both personal and professional, speeches, writings and interviews. That an individual always and essentially belongs to a larger community is a belief he holds right from his childhood and is explicitly seen when he repeatedly writes to his father about his involvement in the family enterprise and the responsibility expected of him. The strong emphasis on the duties of the individual in a free world was also an important theme in his writings. Here is an illustration. A student in a seminary studying for priesthood sent JRD a letter where he asked for JRD's views on the individual, God and religion. JRD's reply focused on the nature of the individual. He wrote:

> I certainly give to the individual the highest value in any scheme of things. On no account would I hold that the individual or any particular class of people is expendable in the interest of any cause however important, and certainly not for personal gain. Any society consists of individuals and should promote the welfare of all with particular emphasis on the weaker elements. This does not mean that the individual has not himself responsibilities towards society.

JRD concluded the letter by writing, 'With best wishes for the success of your studies and your future career as a priest in which, I hope, you will always fight for understanding and brotherhood and against narrow parochialism and hostility to one's fellowman based on religious differences.'[3]

What is equally important for JRD was the sense of responsibility which he expected of the public. If the individual has to have a sense of responsibility and awareness of the larger public then the public also has to show some sense of responsibility towards the individual. This formulation had a significant influence on JRD as far as the public–private relationship was concerned.

I think it is wrong to read JRD only as remarking on the public–private relationship in the business domain. JRD was doing much more; he was bringing the ideas of private and public drawn from the experiences of our individual lives in a social world. He repeatedly emphasised the responsibility of not just the individual but also of the private, whether they are private communities or private companies. These private entities have a responsibility towards the public. This sense of responsibility of the private towards the public is what leads him to consider issues such as social responsibility and social audit.

For a major part of his life, JRD had to conduct his business in a milieu defined by a socialist government. He lived at a time where the role of the government was seen to be essential for the benefit of the nation. Government took on the role of the protector, of an agent which had to control the base desires of private enterprise. JRD felt the brunt of this interventionist mode of governing when his private airline was nationalised. Over the decades, there had also been sporadic demands for nationalisation of the steel industry, particularly catalysed by the success of Tata Steel. Furthermore, the expansion plans of the Tata group were stymied by many government rules. JRD's response to all this reflected his frustration that the government did not understand what was best for the country. It is worthwhile noting that his criticism of the socialist enterprise was based on his view that a system which could not emancipate the poor was fundamentally unsound. For JRD, private enterprise working along ethical principles and with the help of a responsible government had this capacity. He did not envision a State with only private enterprises as he felt that there were sectors where the government had to play a leading role. His frustration was largely with the government's inability to allow the growth of private enterprise, even for those enterprises which had consistently shown a record of exemplary social and stakeholder responsibility.

Many of JRD's views on the role of the government and of the public in general have been borne out by various trends today. On the one hand, there persists a feeling in the general populace that the government is the agency to take care of their problems, whether it be infrastructural issues, generating jobs or even guaranteeing employment. For JRD, the problem with the government was that it was not equipped to deal with this vast job in an efficient manner. His belief that private companies had an obligation which went beyond their profit-making functions made him and his group the pioneers in various innovations with regard to labour policies. For example, Tata Steel introduced labour welfare schemes over the years long before any other company did, including government companies. In fact, many of these initiatives were later formulated as labour laws by the government. These are listed in the next chapter.

JRD's strong belief that a company had to be responsive to the local community was transformed into various programmes designed for the surrounding communities and funded by the companies. For example, today there are three departments within Tata Steel which take cares of urban, semi-urban and peri-urban problems. A significant percentage of the after-tax income of Tata Steel is spent on welfare programmes. An appreciable amount is spent on supporting sporting activities. For example, the Tata Football Academy and the support given to archery are worthwhile mentioning. The archery programme not only enables athletes in the region, where there is a traditional strength in archery, to be trained to world-class levels but also generates employment to these youth and creates a support system for their communities.

In so doing, JRD illustrated the nature of giving – not merely giving but the importance of 'giving back'. Sometimes what he did had a touch of the government! For example, the Tata Football Academy has professional coaches to train the best talent in the country who are chosen after a variety of tests. These students are housed in a comfortable hostel and their diet is specially designed for them by nutritionists. There is a gym as well as a special sports medicine facility. They are also enrolled in a school so that they have a degree when they finish their training. It is important to note that the academy is run like a professional, private academy like many others in the world. The only difference is the enormous fees one would usually have to pay to attend one of those academies, whereas the Tata academy is run by the company and offers scholarships to the students. After their graduation, the students are free to take up any offer they get. The success of the programme is clearly illustrated when we look at the roster of the clubs that these students have joined, and moreover with huge salaries! In the free support given to these students, this Football Academy is doing something that the government has tried to do for various sports. However, it is well known that in these government sports facilities, such as the sports institutes, although there is a good amount of money spent on them, the facilities for the athletes and sportspersons are dismal.

What JRD saw as social responsibility is what is now reflected in the emphasis on decentralised governance, programmes to support growth in rural areas and eradication of poverty not through centralised governmental means but through local action. Shifting the responsibility of taking care of citizens from the government to the private sector is an ideologically important step, especially in the current world of globalisation and free trade. As JRD always maintained, companies had as much of a moral responsibility to lessen the economic deprivation of the local community as the government did, or perhaps even more than the government. He maintained that the major task of private enterprise was not to solve the problems of society but at the same time did not think that removing the abysmal level of poverty in the country was the responsibility of the government alone. It was also not the duty of the Tatas alone but of every person in the country. If there was any facet of the country that troubled JRD till his end it was this degrading poverty of so many of its people.

Having analysed some of the aspects of the nature of private and public, an analysis that is essential to understanding JRD, I would like to explore three themes which JRD repeatedly emphasised. These are the themes of autonomy, account-ability and power/control. All these themes are also related to our understanding of the private/public binary.

Autonomy and accountability

In a broadcast on All India Radio in October 1970, JRD said that the 'problem lies in the fact that autonomy must co-exist with accountability.'[4] The problem arises mainly due to the fact that autonomy and accountability seem to be independent and exclusive of each other. For JRD, the right balance between the two was what was so problematic in practice. His response to this problem is revealing. He noted that autonomy 'cannot emanate from a Parliamentary statute alone. It must come also from a voluntary abdication and delegation of powers by those who hold power initially.'[5] This solution is very important as it brings into the notion of accountability the idea of voluntary abdication. The resonance with Gandhi's demand of voluntary abdication of political power, particularly by the Congress party, should not be overlooked here. Although JRD uttered these sentiments in the context of autonomy in the public sector, we can see a consistent pattern to his thought in various other contexts regarding this issue. In the case of the public sector, JRD, unlike what might be commonly believed of private industrialists, believed in the importance of the public sector, which included, for him, its use in fulfilling 'social obligations'. He maintained that the 'public sector has a great role to play in the economic development of the country.'[6] In the case of the public sector, JRD was arguing for greater autonomy for employees and less interference from the government on all matters pertaining to the management of the public sector. He also took a similar view in the context of accountability of private industries to the larger society, both in terms of support to the local community and the nation, and to various kinds of intellectual activities such as academics or art.

The idea of autonomy is related to ideas such as freedom, independence, creativity and so on. Autonomy indicates various capacities such as the capacity to explore, be creative and reach the potential of one's capabilities. At its foundations it is no more than the freedom to act according to one's wishes and desires with no answerability to others. The issue of autonomy is present even in our daily lives and personal relationships, and not just in the context of private or public industries. However, the fundamental problem is that the idea of autonomy attempts to isolate an individual being whereas fundamentally we function, almost always, as social beings, meaning thereby that we are always beholden to others. We are a by-product of the imagination of other people, whether it be our parents, teachers, friends or even strangers. We create our lives by responding to the stimuli around us. We are not independent beings, independent neither of the world or the society in which we find ourselves. However, we are also not one cog in the machine, totally dictated by the social. What distinguishes the idea of the human, of the individual, is the ability to stand alone, to have a conscious will that can go against the dictates of the world and society.

This perennial tension about doing what we want, what our conscious will and desire demand of us, and of being part of a larger world is one of the most enervating ones. JRD's response to this issue, I presume, would have been to emphasise the importance of local autonomy in the sense that we can only attempt to do our best given that we are forever forced to work under circumstances that may not be the most ideal. The tension with accountability comes to the fore only when it impedes our capacity to do our best in a given set of circumstances, when the objective towards which our action is directed is itself harmed by the constraining mechanisms.

The deeper question here is of moral autonomy and accountability. I am not talking about personal morality here. The very notion of a private individual, the very force of the utterance 'I', is a statement of individual, private autonomy. Who can the private individual be accountable to? In a religious world, where God plays a regulating role, individuals may perhaps be accountable to God. But in a secular universe, who can we be accountable to? The paradox is that pure autonomy is meaningless. We can understand JRD as holding the belief that one can be autonomous when one best knows the limits of one's accountability. Freedom to act was of paramount importance to him. Once an action is agreed upon, based on the constraints of autonomy and accountability, then the individual must be free to act upon it.

Accountability is not just to an external agency like the government but also to oneself, and by extension to one's community, nation and the world in various differing ways. Thus, we can distinguish JRD's ideas as articulating two modes of accountability: personal and public or internal and external. How can we be accountable to oneself? This question is of central importance to the larger ethical world of JRD. In a letter, he wrote that 'I believe that democratic freedoms are an inalienable birthright only when accompanied by self-imposed discipline and obligations to the society and the country in which one lives.'[7]

His views on the role of the private sector illustrate his approach to the problem of accountability. He believed that corruption, black marketing, evasion of taxes, bribery etc. by private companies had contributed to a perception that private companies were essentially concerned only with personal gain at the expense of everything else. Right from the beginning of his involvement in the Tata empire, JRD looked for ways to express the social consciousness of their business, a consciousness which was initiated by the vision of the founding fathers.

JRD expressed this vision clearly in many of his speeches. Two of them, one in 1969 and another in 1970, illustrate this particularly well. In a talk on the public sector he emphasised the need for autonomy in the public sector.[8] And, interestingly, in the speech dealing with the private sector he underlined the need for accountability![9] The demand for accountability in the private domain and autonomy in the public domain was a constant and essential theme for JRD. In the talk on the public sector he argued that autonomy 'carried to an extreme would totally frustrate the principle of accountability, while accountability also carried to an extreme would totally nullify the concept of autonomy. Determining the right mid-point between the two extremes is what has been found so difficult to achieve in practice'. He further pointed out that we needed more than legislation to make autonomy possible. In the beginning of this section, I referred to his belief that autonomy would come from voluntary abdication of power. The idea of 'voluntary abdication' is an important one for JRD. In the case of the public sector, he wanted the government to learn to handle its power in a responsible manner. This responsibility includes making the public sector efficient. He also argued that government presence in the management of public-sector enterprises was important since they would make sure that social obligations were fulfilled by these enterprises. We can clearly see JRD's hope that not only will the private sector learn to be socially responsible but also that the public sector should be involved in such activities.

In the speech about the private sector, he suggested that private enterprise must voluntarily set up social audit, an idea that has become popular in recent times. Among other responsibilities of the private sector, he mentioned the following: setting up charitable Trusts; support for relief and reconstruction measures; support the communities in which their business interests are situated, in particular to help those even if they do not work in their companies by providing schools, dispensaries, roads and such like; support of the local economy by purchasing local goods from the local community; sending their engineers and doctors to spend some time in social service. JRD was also very clear that such betterment of the surroundings was not only good for the community around the industry but it was also good for the industry. He believed that in the early decades after Independence there was a great suspicion of private enterprise by the government and that, therefore, there was also a need 'to show ourselves worthy of the trust placed in us.'[10]

A measure of this accountability was also reflected in his support for the mixed economy, an economy in which public and private sectors function together. In September 1953, in the Chairman's Statement of TISCO, JRD clarified the nature of a mixed economy in terms of a 'balance of forces, with free enterprise operating as one of the autonomous forces pulling its weight alongside State enterprises, trade unions and other elements in society.'[11] We should remember that it was from 1 August 1953 that the government nationalised private airlines and JRD's statement is soon after this event, by all accounts a shattering one for JRD, as the government took over not just his airline company, which he had nurtured and built with great love, but also intruded into his love affair with aviation. He accepted that he was not demanding a totally free-market economy and added that the 'interests of the nation as a whole must prevail over the interests of the few.'[12] An important consequence of a balance thus established would be in helping to 'instil in the private sector the sense of trusteeship advocated by Mahatma Gandhi and would put squarely upon it the responsibility for placing national above sectional and personal interests.'[13] In the last chapter I discussed the notion of the greater good. JRD's claim that the interests of the nation must prevail over that of a few indicates this particular ethical principle which informed his understanding of the private sector in our country. The themes of balance and trusteeship, which I believe were two of the most influential themes in JRD's philosophy, will be discussed in greater detail in the next chapter.

Power and control

A related theme, discernible in bits and parts in JRD's writings, but one that is very influential in understanding the notions of accountability and autonomy, is that of power. Related to the idea of power is that of control. These themes of power and control are important philosophical themes, especially in the context of human existence and human relationships. Manifestation of power is clearly seen in both private and public domains. I will discuss this issue mainly in order to explore the boundaries of autonomy and accountability, and the various ways in which they manifest themselves.

There is a simple question that we can begin with. Is autonomy a measure of the power one wields? Or, equivalently, a measure of the lack of restriction on the power one could wield? The problem of wielding power or learning to wield power is related to two important themes that were essential to the larger worldview of JRD. One is that of responsibility, especially necessary when one has power. The other is the greater theme of control, whether it is of one's desires or ambition, whether of a private or public entity. Control is also related to responsibility in that certain kinds of control, such as controlling one's ambition to succeed at the cost of everything else, is part of the responsibility of the individual to use the power wisely. To paraphrase JRD, we can only be trustees of the power that is given to us when we acquire a position where we inherit some power.

JRD's emphasis on responsibility, as mentioned above, can be explicated further using the notion of control. Philosophers and psychologists have long understood the primordial importance of the idea of control in our lives. In the way we deal with others and even with ourselves, we invoke the notion of control all the time. Control has both positive and negative connotations. It has long been an accepted presupposition of human societies that humans have to be controlled. Social and moral laws are most often based on the assumption that without some form of control over human action it will be impossible to have a society. The implication here is that we are essentially individual beings with personal interest dictating all our actions. In a group, sacrifice of personal interest is necessary and there is a strong belief that given a choice an individual would not make such a sacrifice. This can only be accomplished by the introduction of various kinds of norms, such as social and ethical norms of behaviour. Therefore, as far as the social is concerned, control is the mechanism for regulating individual, private behaviour.

Control is also an important element in the life of an individual. Controlling oneself or self-control is one of the privileged virtues extolled in most religious and ethical texts. The argument in this case is that control is no doubt necessary but that is not to be imposed by any outside agency. It is the individual who decides – thereby exercising her conscious will – to control her desires, ambition and action. Almost any ethical discourse will have elements of self-control. If we look at any of the great mythological stories or in contemporary times Gandhi's experiments with controlling his desire, we can see the importance of the idea of self-control. Often, society does not trust the individual enough to leave the matter of control to the individual herself. The imposition of social norms (including ethical ones) is a mechanism to make sure that if the individual does not exhibit control, society will.

As humans living in and as part of a society, there is an intrinsic idea of control. It is this idea that defines some basic elements of human civilisation. To control our anger and our behaviour is the first lesson of social behaviour; controlling our emotions in 'public' reflects the role that control plays in presenting ourselves to others. The Buddhist credo to control our desires, a moral injunction that is reflected in many spiritual traditions including that of Gandhi, understands the activity of control as being essential to what is human in us.

In the context of material wealth, there is always an undercurrent of moral judgement against its accumulation. Greed has for long been a favourite sin. Capitalism, in principle, has to negotiate with the notion of greed. The problem is compounded when greed and profit are often understood to be closely related. While it is true that private enterprise has shown a proclivity to accumulate wealth and has many members who can in all fairness be called greedy, there is also a need to distinguish between profit and greed. Controlling greed has always been a part of ethical discourse, both at the individual and societal level.

It is useful to recollect here JRD's concern about the nature of capitalism. In a letter where he discussed labour, socialism and capitalism, he noted how capitalism could be misused and because of which controls were needed. He argued that the problem with socialism and the State was that they were not democratic, thus leading him to echo what he said in other fora, namely that economic totalitarianism will also lead to political totalitarianism. He concluded by pointing out that the Yugoslav model in which workers become owners was a good model and that 'labour must somehow or other be permitted gradually to share in the responsibilities of management.' He thought that the illiteracy of Indian labour was the major hindrance towards making this model possible.[14]

Businesses also invoke the notion of control in many different ways. For example, control of resources is an important component of business practice. It is now more appropriate to rename 'control' as 'manage', as in managing resources or managing people. This notion of managing exhibits many of the characteristics of the notion of control.

Control is an important component of human relations and emotions. As is well known, even children use emotions as a means of control. Adults engage with it all the time. In personal behaviour, control is exhibited in many activities and it has a wide variety of meanings. Parents control children's behaviour by invoking their authority to stop a child from behaving in a particular manner. Spouses use various mechanisms of control, derived both from their personal action and also from social norms, in interpersonal relationships. In fact, if there is something universal in human relationships, it is the manifestation of control. Thus, it is no surprise that philosophers such as those belonging to the Existentialist school have been able to gain deep philosophical insight into the nature of the human by analysing the idea of control.

Modern societies and capitalism, based as they are on the growth of the scientific, technological enterprise, have an essential relationship with control. Primarily, we can trace it back to the centrality of the notion of control that is necessary for establishing the scientific worldview. Philosophers have long been aware that one of the most important characteristics of modern science is its capacity to control the world, both its resources and the various phenomena of nature. Control is essential to science in that without the possibility of control there can be no experiments. The very possibility of quantitative measurement and replicability of experiments is very much dependent on the amount of control a scientist has over the phenomena. Technology has an intrinsic relation to control, and thus capitalism, which flourished under the influence of modern technology, is intrinsically related to the theme of control.

JRD responded to the problem of control, not in terms of these theoretical paradigms but more at an experiential level. He felt the injustice of control, especially needless control by bureaucrats and politicians. He saw this control as a manifestation of improper use of power. In one of his speeches he referred to the 'psychology of power which motivates people', that made them exercise their power in the following ways: 'power of control and patronage, power to delay an application, power to hold up a file, power to keep people waiting in an ante-room, all of which are consciously or subconsciously treated as symbols of prestige and hallmarks of importance.'[15] He went on to add, lest we think that this was his imagination at work, that this was told to him privately by a leading bureaucrat.

He was particularly anguished at the use of power and control to harass people. Writing about the growth and strength of bureaucracy, he conjectured that in the years to come (and he thought it would be by the year 2000) bureaucrats would have tied up everything in red tape. And he wickedly added: 'If I am reborn I hope I will end up as a bureaucrat!'[16]

In his own case, he was often dismissive of the mistaken belief that corporates wielded enormous economic power. In a meeting with the Planning Commission in 1968, he attacked the myth of economic power supposedly concentrated in a few individuals/groups. He sarcastically said, 'As I wake up every morning, I carefully consider to what purpose I shall apply my great powers that day. Shall I crush competitors, exploit consumers, fire recalcitrant workers, topple a Government or two?'[17] He went on to add that this was a myth propagated by those who were opposed to any private enterprise. Further, he pointed out that economic power was actually monopolised in the hands of government officials. And what he said in the Chairman's Statement of TISCO in 1972 is quite telling.

> Deprived of the right to decide what and how much to produce, what prices to charge, how much to borrow, what shares to issue and at what price, what wages and bonus to pay, what executives to employ and what salaries to pay them and in some cases, what dividends to distribute, directors and top Management from the Chairman down hardly have any economic power in our country. Taking my own case, I doubt that there is anywhere in the world outside India any industrial executive in charge of a major enterprise with less real power than I have. In fact, no Government in the world has taken greater precautions to ensure that real economic power is removed from Management's hands and is concentrated on its own.[18]

Control and power are synonymous in many contexts. Control can be exerted only when one has power to do so. The problem about control is whether power necessarily implies control. That is, can one have power and yet not exert any control? This question is indeed central to the question of power and control, whether in private lives or public institutions. JRD's observations echo what millions of common citizens routinely experience and voice. We know that the bureaucrats' power consists in their capacity to make us feel powerless in front of them. Right from the peon onwards, this percolation of power and control has been the single most frustrating obstacle in the creation of a sensitive ruling class. I am drawing attention to this point only to make a link between the uses of power in the private and public domains.

Control is an essential theme in JRD's way of looking not just at industry or economics but also in the way he understands the world and perhaps even personal relations. Control as a concept is important for JRD because the fundamental impulse of responsibility arises from our awareness of the need to control something or the other. Responsible individual behaviour is itself a manifestation of successful control.

How do we address this issue of power? Is it possible to build societies where there is no hierarchy with differential powers distributed across it? Or is it by nature that we are hierarchical and our society also similarly constructed? Dumont's description of humans as *homo hierarchicus* is influential in social thought but the question that is relevant here is whether our social ordering necessarily reflects hierarchy. This issue is important because if our personal and public lives are structured along the gradients of power then we need to find ways to deal with it. Social ordering of power cannot reflect the personal gradation of it.

Let me consider two possible responses to the wielding of power: resistance and responsibility. One can resist unjust use of power through various forms of protest and resistance. The other response to power comes from the person who has the power invested in him or her. And this response, one tinged with ethical humanism, is to exercise responsibility in the use of the power granted to an individual.

Is there a different paradigm to understand power and control? JRD's thoughts and actions suggest that he would have liked to rephrase these notions in terms of 'freedom and responsibility'. Freedom and power are related in an essential manner. Power is manifested only through the freedom to act according to one's desire. We can use our power in many different ways, one of which is to use it as a mechanism of control. For JRD, the idea of power was important since power also grants us the capacity to make meaningful changes but power comes with responsibility. The greater power one has, the greater the responsibility.

Finally, it is important to note that JRD's notion of control is not about control of human desires. In contrast, he loved a good life, in that the very act of living exemplified a great spirit, which embraced the possibility of being challenged and of overcoming those challenges. This view set him apart from a dominant stream in discourse on control where self-control, especially the control of one's desires, was highly valued.

Responsibility is indeed an important theme for JRD. But what exactly does it mean to be responsible? When can we evaluate whether we are being responsible in a given situation? How much responsibility should we hold? These and related questions are deeply related to one of the most important ideas that drives businesses, namely, profit. The next chapter will discuss the need for an expanded notion of profit through which philanthropy becomes an actual part of business.

Notes

1 R. M. Lala. *The Joy of Achievement: Conversations with J.R.D. Tata*. New Delhi: Viking, 1995, pp. 71–72.
2 For more details, see Guru, G. and S. Sarukkai, *Experience, Caste and the Everyday Social*, New Delhi: Oxford University Press, 2019.
3 Letter to Brother Joseph Puthenpura, 30 April 1973.
4 J. R. D. Tata. *Keynote*. Edited by S. A. Sabavala and R. M. Lala. Bombay: Tata Press Limited, 1986, p. 37.
5 Ibid., p. 37.
6 Ibid., p. 38.

7 Letter to Dastur, 18 February 1977. It is unfortunate that he wrote this in the context of Emergency. JRD was taken to have supported the Emergency or at least supported one consequence of Emergency, namely, the inculcation of discipline in the society. JRD in later years accepted that this support was one of the biggest mistakes in his life.
8 *Keynote*, op. cit., p. 37.
9 Ibid., p. 40.
10 *Keynote*, op. cit., p. 48.
11 Ibid., p. 46.
12 Ibid., p. 47.
13 Ibid., p. 47.
14 Letter to Daji, May 1955.
15 *Keynote*, op. cit., p. 65.
16 Letter to Dr Carl Gerstacker, Michigan, 17 August 1977.
17 *Keynote*, op. cit., p. 62.
18 Ibid., p. 68.

6

PROFIT

JRD once recollected an encounter with Nehru, where he told Nehru that the 'public sector was badly run' and that 'it should make a profit for the country'. Hearing this, Nehru became angry and told JRD, 'Don't talk to me about that dirty word profit.'[1]

Nehru's response to the idea of profit was not an exception; it was shared by a large community of politicians and intellectuals who felt that profit was a dirty word. That was perhaps a sign of the times in which they lived. Or perhaps it was a sign of the times to come; fifty-odd years later, profit has become a desirable word.

Profit has been the engine of the business enterprise from time immemorial. Over the ages, many different meanings have been attached to it, some of which have fallen by the wayside and others which have been reinforced so much so that, today, profit is largely understood in a narrow sense of the word.

JRD, as a businessman, was well aware of the importance of profit although he spent his life trying to expand its meaning beyond its narrow materialist definition. To understand JRD and his ethics of business, it will be useful to begin this chapter with the notion of profit. But in doing this, like in other themes related to JRD's view of business and life, I will outline the contours of his thoughts and actions, and expand on them using not only the insights he had about these themes but also drawing upon some basic ideas needed for his formulations. JRD was a man of action and although not a theorist was a man of reflection. One of the most important ideas from which it is worthwhile to begin is that of profit and JRD's attempt to open the notion of profit to the challenges of a humanist society.

The first section in the chapter analyses some aspects of JRD's notion of profit, primarily the need to have an expanded view of profit. To understand the various issues involved in JRD's view of profit, we have to consider the nature of profit and what it really means. The second section discusses various analyses of the nature of profit, which may help us reflect on JRD's views in a more informed manner. This discussion will also explore the different presuppositions inherent in this simple idea of profit, which will hopefully set the ground for a deeper engagement with certain aspects of profit, those that were of particular concern to JRD. Following this, I will discuss JRD's attempts to enlarge the meaning of profit by including factors such as profit for many, profit for the future and profit for the community. In so doing, JRD was bringing in notions of qualitative profit within the dominant paradigm that viewed profit dominantly in quantitative terms. Further, there is an important relation between ownership and profit. JRD's views on ownership are extremely interesting and I discuss some aspects of them while analysing the question of who owns the profits. Once the idea of profit is enriched by including various qualitative measures, the uses of profit and the 'right' means towards profit will appear naturally in any analysis of profit.

JRD's view of profit

Profit is not restricted to monetary or material profit alone. We profit in many different ways. For JRD, it is this more complex sense of profit that is of great importance. We can understand little of his actions if we cannot place them within his more universal view of profit and the means of attaining it.

The idea of profit is basic to any definition of business. Although JRD was a man of many interests and broad vision, he was foremost a businessman. But he was also a very different kind of businessman. Some of what he did and wrote on business placed him in opposition to how other business entrepreneurs viewed themselves. This is especially true of his views on the creation and use of profit. JRD did not believe that business corporations were in the business of charity; he believed that profit, efficiency and growth were important parameters for their existence. In fact, he more than once argued that making profits was the way to generate resources for social welfare. Thus, the problem is not in making profits per se but in knowing how one makes profits and how one uses them.

However, there is also another idea of profit that is commonly available in JRD's writings and action. This has to do with the broader notion of profit whereby one profits not only materially but also through certain ethical practices; through expansion of the cultural space of an individual's mind, for instance through music and education; through a humane approach towards fellow citizens etc. Profit is thus also profiting of the mind, the body, tradition, culture, community and nation. JRD's notion of profit is not restrictive, such as one focused entirely either on material and monetary profit or on personal profit.

It would be useful to discuss two extensions of JRD's basic formulation. One is the idea of profitability *for many* and the other is profitability *for the future*. In small businesses, profit belongs to the individual who owns the business. In larger companies, profit is shared between the owners and the shareholders. In the standard view of sharing profit, the beneficiaries are all those who own the company in part or in full. JRD expands this traditional way of viewing profit to include the ideas of 'profit for many' and 'profit for the future'. This approach has a resonance with ethical ideas of the 'greater good'. Many ethical principles of justice and governance, including the democratic ideal, are based on the idea of the greater good and bringing profit into this discourse expands the ethical issues in the nature and use of profit. The essential point here is that profit should be made to work for a larger set of people, including those who do not have any direct stakeholdership in the business that makes the profit, for instance, shareholders of a public company. Similarly, profit for the future is using profit to benefit a larger number of people not only in the immediate aftermath of earning profit but establishing institutions such that the profit is distributed over time. So, both these ideas are attempts to make profit do more work both across space and time.

The emphasis on the distribution of profit such that it spreads over future generations is one that is clearly seen in the emphasis on institution building. In the case of Jamsetji Tata, the founder of the Tata enterprise, it was clearly manifested in his vision for the creation of the Indian Institute of Science for which he set aside not only a significant part of his personal wealth but also put in extraordinary effort to get this institute going, especially when there was some early reluctance on the part of the British authorities. This capacity to extend the idea of profit beyond the immediate confines of the entrepreneur or beyond the confines of his or her lifetime indicates the idea of profit as a dynamic concept, one whose applicability is extended across space and time. The creation of various Trusts such as the Sir Dorabji Tata Trust, Sir Ratan Tata Trust and JRD Tata Trust is an illustration of this wider vision.

Understanding profit within the discourse of the greater good, a value which is accessible not only to the entrepreneur but also to the various stakeholders in the concern such as its employees, local community and the nation, immediately and automatically regulates the means by which profit is made. In fact, the emphasis on the quantitative measure of profit has served to veil the important problem of how profit is created. This de-linking of profit from the ways by which it is produced is one of the main reasons why profit has been seen by some to be a 'dirty' word. In a traditional view of business, profit was the end-all of business, the aim of doing business as it were. Since profit was the only aim of engaging in business and was exclusively the property of the 'owner' of the business, the question of how the profit was made became relatively unimportant. If the bottom line is profit then there is the possibility of using various forms of exploitation to achieve a profit. In the labour movement, it was often felt that exploitation of labour was condoned in the name of profit and hence the word 'profit' became an anathema not only to the socialist and communist movements but also to leaders such as Nehru whose reaction to profit was mentioned at the beginning of this chapter.

However, if profit is placed within the discourse of the greater good, such as profit for many or profit for the future, then it is immediately answerable to some ethical issues and thus becomes part of a larger ethical universe. The resistance of many businesses to engage with a more serious evaluation of the idea of profit is largely a resistance to place it within an ethical domain. But, for JRD, the whole issue of profit is tied not only to the idea of a greater good but also to the means of creating profit. Above all else, JRD was very clear about the strictures to be placed on these means. I would venture to suggest here that for JRD the most important concern was the means of creating profit and unless the means were 'clean' the profit too would not be 'clean'. JRD took great pride in the cleanliness of the Tata companies, especially in the context of corruption and various other unfair practices. This was a theme he repeatedly talked about and as far as we can see in his actions, letters and speeches, he forcefully demanded fairness in practice, not only from his own organisation but also from other business concerns. It is important to note that he demanded this fairness from the government and its representatives too. Since ethical issues are by definition more universal, demanding fair methods of creating profit makes a private business concern a 'public' entity. This was a conclusion which JRD explicitly held – that although companies were privately owned, they were also accountable just like the government.

The greatest damage to the image of business arises in the wake of privileging profit over everything else. In India, we have seen large-scale exploitation of land, resources, people and government for the personal benefits of businesses. In so doing, there is great complicity among many people, including those in the private and government sectors. JRD's demand for fair means meant that he was forever fighting against an established group with connections among the rich and powerful. Although he was himself a distinguished member of the business community, he repeatedly gave vent to his frustration about some sections of the community going beyond fair means in order to grow. He made these comments when asked about some business concerns flourishing under certain governments. He also expressed these reservations strongly when there were problems of large-scale evasion of taxes and black marketing in the country. It is important to note that JRD made these views of his public, and in so doing was making himself and his organisation accountable to counter charges. It is not surprising that charges of tax evasion were brought upon one or two Tata companies, but on the other hand it is also a matter of great surprise that so few charges of unfair practice have been made against the Tata group. JRD could voice these concerns and demand more ethical practices mainly because he was confident that his companies were not indulging in any of these practices. Thus, his conviction and strength came from what he saw was the cleanliness of his organisation.

Once profit is placed within a broader domain, once it is answerable to a host of factors which go beyond the benefit to an individual or a small group of owners, then the nature of profit immediately changes. For example, Jamsetji Tata believed that what was needed for the nation were steel and power industries along with a technical institute. Thus, it can be argued that the decision to start these organisations was not wholly concerned with profitability seen in a narrow sense since the motivation for the creation of these industries was more than mere material profit. However, in the broader meaning of profit, the creation of these companies and institute was of great profit to the nation. Power and steel were very important for the infrastructural capabilities of a nation which needed them in its industrialisation process and the institute was an infrastructure for quality education of its citizens. In an interview much later in life, JRD notes that most of the companies started by the Tatas were chosen in those sectors that would benefit the national infrastructure. The implication of this is that new businesses started by this group were not based on considerations of monetary profits alone. But neither are any of these concerns a charity in the sense that they are gifts with no accountability attached to them.

This was an important point as far as JRD was concerned. Creating institutions, whether they are companies, hospitals, research institutes or Trusts alone, is not enough. A sense of responsibility and accountability must continue to be present even when JRD or the Tatas had no direct role in the institutions they created. What they succeeded in doing by expanding the meaning of profit was to make profit accountable and answerable to various other factors.

We can now discern various themes inherent in JRD's view of profit which can be analysed in greater detail, some aspects of which are discussed in the following section. Firstly, it is clear that the notion of profit for JRD had to have an expanded form and must include various themes such as ownership, responsibility, fair practice and the greater good. Secondly, although JRD may not have articulated it exactly in this fashion, he saw business in a holistic sense in that the universe of a business included a host of factors which were not traditionally seen as belonging to the responsibilities of business. Thirdly, he was a pragmatist and his adaptability arises from the pragmatic instinct. However, it must be noted that his insistence on certain ethical guidelines of conduct meant that pragmatism was no back door for escaping ethical responsibilities.

The meaning of profit

The word 'profit' is actually associated with many different meanings, including material gain. Other usages of the word, some of them by now obsolete, are proficiency, advancement and improvement, to progress, to prosper, improve, and so on. Prospering materially was only one of these many meanings.

However, there is a complexity to the idea of profit that can be usefully explored. In the most general sense, to profit is to be able to generate more than what is given or available. More refined views of profit will fine-tune this definition but for our purposes it is useful to start with this common-sense view of profit. Paradoxically, this simple notion of profit illustrates two contradictory natural principles. One is that of conservation, which is manifested not only in the laws of physics but also in the activities of our daily life, and the other is related to the capacity of human reason. A common principle which we often invoke is 'there is no gain or loss'. Or, 'what is gained is lost somewhere else'. This is well embodied in the principle of conservation of mass, according to which the total mass energy before an event is the same after the event. In common experience, when an object is broken, we believe that all the pieces of the object must equal the mass of the object before it was broken. That is, in a physical act, mass cannot just vanish into nothingness. This is reflective of an important principle of equilibrium. This is indeed a universal principle in that it holds across a vast domain. To be in a state of equilibrium is to accept that all actions are part of a complex zero-sum game. In this worldview, to indulge in an activity that generates profit, which by its very meaning generates something more than what is put in, will in turn cause a loss somewhere else thereby retaining a total equilibrium around this activity. To put it crudely, if we make money in a particular act, then somebody else loses that amount or its equivalent. Such a view informs the position that profit is a 'dirty' word because of the belief that there is no way in which one can make more out of something without it being lost by somebody else.

There are many nuanced arguments that can support such a view. For example, monetary profit may be offset by factors such as loss of resources, environmental degradation or various forms of pollution. Thus, even though a company might make profit there could have been a corresponding loss in many other sectors. The emphasis on the 'many' is important and is more tenable than the view which would claim that a profit at one point leads to a loss in another. Such a singular causation is quite improbable. What happens in practice, even in this model of equilibrium, is that profit in one region may be distributed as costs to many regions instead of just one. In other words, while profit may peak at one point, the corresponding loss may be distributed across a wider range. This is, of course, a more sympathetic view of profit and the cost of profiting.

This approach to profit is also related to the more interesting issue of holism. More than any other human activity, business is part of a large web consisting not just of an individual or a company but a web of relations including communities, consumers, stakeholders and the world. It can perhaps be argued that there are other individual human activities which are not that explicitly part of a larger web as is business since a business is essentially a public activity. For example, a business is always involved in a relation with consumers. These consumers belong to particular socio-cultural communities and thus business is engaged in a relationship with this larger community. Since the very act of business is involved thus in a web, it is but natural to believe that doing something to one part of the web disturbs another part. This, therefore, suggests that a gain in one region of the web leads to a loss in another. However, this is a limited view of business and profit. While this view may be partly true, there is also another way of looking at these activities, which is through the metaphor of the growth of organisms.

Before discussing this issue further, consider the other contradictory natural principle. Such a principle is central to the very capacity of human reason, which so strikingly illustrates the capacity to take something given to us in perception and add to it an input much beyond the simple perception. For example, to see a blue bird and understand a concept such as the colour blue is itself an example of the capacity of human reason to see more than what is given to our perception. Thus, reason is that which illustrates the capacity to increase the given. In a strict sense then, human reason reflects the profit of the human mind, a profit it makes out of its experiences with the world. For example, we make various kinds of inferences;

generalisations are one of our most common mental acts. Generalisations are an indicator of this 'mercantile' nature of reason because by seeing a few incidents we are able to generalise it to many unobserved instances, including predictions of such instances in the future. One might want to understand this as indicative of an economy of reason, whereby thinking is made more economically viable because of this capacity to generalise. Whatever may be the explanations, we see an important 'natural' correlation to the idea of profit as enlarging upon what is originally available.

However, not all increase captures the sense of profit since there could be increases which are caused by the addition of various factors. Building something is to increase from what we began with but it is not a materially profitable activity and, in fact, is quite the opposite since we spend money to build. However, there is also a notion of profitability attached to spending money to build a house. This common example illustrates the inherent problems in understanding profit in any restricted sense.

Therefore, there are two natural phenomena that manifest two opposing sides of the profit divide. One side would imply that there can never be anything like profit without a concomitant loss somewhere else. On the other hand, like human reason, the capacity to expand upon the given is something that is uniquely human. So, perhaps we can consider the possibility that the tendency towards profiting is very much a human trait whereas the tendency towards equilibrium and equivalence is the trait of the natural world.

There is another biological metaphor to help us understand the nature of profit and this is the metaphor of growth of an organism. From a given state the organism develops in various ways, enlarging upon the initial state. But for such growth to be possible, there needs to be nurturing and sustenance. In the equilibrium view, the net increment seen in growth will be balanced by the various elements that are added to the input to make something grow. So, strictly speaking, there is no 'net' profit in this sense. However, there is a crucial difference. An organism has to grow and without growth there is death. Therefore, growth is not a choice. If we understand business concerns in this organic way, then they perforce have to grow and once they stop growing they die. On the other hand, there is no growth possible without a concomitant presence of profit. In other words, without profit there is no growth and without growth there is no life to the company or business. Therefore, the biological metaphor of organism makes profit an essential component of all businesses. Once profit is seen as being essential to the very existence of business, then it might perhaps cease to be a dirty word. Such an organic view of business is often found in the everyday talk of those engaged in business.

However, we should note an important problem in this approach. The problem here would be to define what we mean by growth, even growth of an organism. What are the limits of growth? What is the boundary of growth? Consider this simple example. Suppose we think of an individual who has just been born. How much growth should this individual have? For instance, using height and weight as parameters of growth, we can ask whether this individual should grow to a height of six feet and a weight of 75 kgs in adulthood? Or, if the individual grows only to five feet and weighs 50 kgs does it mean that there is something lacking in her? So, even in the organism picture, it is important to clarify exactly how much growth is desirable. The various measures of human growth in different societies point to the problem of identifying what is ideal growth. It is well known that in all societies the average height has increased over the generations. It is also well known that in rich societies there is in fact an excess weight of individuals due to excessive consumption. The richest countries not only consume a disproportionate amount of resources, including food and power, but also contribute the greatest amount of waste. Thus, while we accept the idea of growth as being integral to an organic picture of business, we also need to know how to determine its parameters and boundaries. Ethics enters this discussion if business by itself cannot rationally determine these boundaries.

To further understand this problem of growth, we can draw upon a theme that occurs not only in philosophy but also in our common wisdom. Using such themes illustrates another useful way of understanding the nature of profit, one which does not necessarily imply that profiting at one level means loss in another. The theme I want to discuss is associated with the idea of potentiality and converting the potential into the actual. Such a picture of growth defined in terms of potential and the actual is common to many philosophical traditions as well as modern biology. It is also one that has had a significant influence in the discourse of business.

The theme can be summarised as follows. An individual has a potential. It is the responsibility of the individual to reach that potential. However, to reach that potential involves dedicated work by the individual, although such dedication is no guarantee that the potential will be reached. But without such dedication there is no possibility of fulfilling the potential of the individual. This image of the individual and the work ethic associated with achieving the potential are one of the most influential images we have of ourselves in contemporary societies. It is no wonder that laziness is anathema in such cultures where reaching the potential is an integral aspect of living. In various representations of modern culture, we can see how this image is established. One powerful way is by making this a duty, an ethical duty of an individual to live up to his or her potential. Ideas such as merit, excellence, professionalism and hard work are related essentially to this demand on the individual to live up to his or her potential.

This ethical view is particularly true of any philosophy which places the human individual at the centre. If the individual is at the centre, as against God or family or society, then it is the individual's ethical duty to do what he or she should since individuals are autonomous beings in this view. Not so surprisingly, capitalism is closely associated with this importance given to individualism. Capitalism privileges, encourages and rewards individual initiative and struggle. Everything else, including governments, is usually seen to be a threat against individual prowess. The celebration of the individual capacity is actually a validation of the gifted individual who is thus given the right and power to do what he or she can best do as an individual. This is also based on the sometimes mistaken assumption that larger groups, including governments, impede human creativity, ambition and drive. Thus, capitalism needs an unfettered individual who can make her dreams come true without inhibition from other factors.

Therefore, growth as a process that exemplifies potentiality is one way to counter the zero-sum view. Making it an ethical principle that an individual should attempt to reach her potentiality makes profiting and growth answerable to some notion of ethical duty. The extension to companies and organisations is obvious. So, we could claim that the primary duty of an organisation is to actualise its potential. Today, much of the talk on evaluation of organisations reflects this comparison between the potential of the organisation and its actual state. In this view, profit is already hidden in the nucleus of the business and everything else is an attempt to manifest this potential profit. The belief that certain businesses are profitable, or liable to make profit in the future, is an illustration of this view that businesses begin with the nucleus of profitability.

The idea of potential is also manifested in those types of business where profit occurs not in terms of material exchange but because of fulfilment of needs. For example, let us suppose that there is a particular need felt by a community and an individual creates a business concern to satisfy those needs. Because of the value in doing this, the entrepreneur might be able to obtain a much higher profit for the service. Thus, the profit arises not because there was a concurrent loss elsewhere but primarily because of the value of that business in the eyes of the people or community. Religious places seen as business concerns also exemplify this view. For example, suppose I construct a temple, which then attracts a large number of devotees. Starting a temple actually satisfies a need in the people and thus, if so desired, there is the possibility of making it profitable. Profit in these kinds of business activities can be understood as a consequence of some potential which has been actualised.[2] In this context, we can note the relationship between a nation's needs and the industries that are started to fulfil these needs. This view was instrumental for Jamsetji and later on for JRD also, both of whom felt that they should create industries which fulfil the needs of the nation. There is a 'profit' in such fulfilment, both material and non-material profit, one that is qualitatively different from profits accruing in various other business activities.

However, even in this approach, there is a problem similar to the ambiguity in knowing what constitutes the potential of an individual. In today's world, we have seen the difficulties in holding a belief that a person should attempt to reach his or her potential. For example, schooling these days is no longer a pleasurable activity of learning but an aggressive competition related to performance. The impact of this is felt through one's life even after schooling is over. The aggressiveness present in jobs, and in the larger society, is a reflection of the fact that we aim to maximise our potential and benefit even at the expense of others. Therefore, just having the idea of the potential in an organism, whether it be the potential of an individual or a business concern, is not enough. What we need to take into account is the actuality associated with this individual entity.

The actual is never the potential. In fact, the potential is always circumscribed by the actual. To illustrate: I may have a potential for doing something but may not be in a position to accomplish it due to various reasons and constraints. How then do we balance the actual with the potential? In other words, what ethical rights do we have in expecting that the potential be realised? Equivalently, we can ask whether a potential should always be maximised. Should we always try to live up to our potential or can we accept that doing our best in the given circumstances is enough? This dilemma is reflected in various ways not only as individuals but also in the profession of business. For example, suppose to live up to my potential as an entrepreneur, I find that I have to neglect my family. Then, we can ask whether living up to my potential as an entrepreneur is more important than accepting the constraints of the actual world, in this case my family. Herein lies the problem with potential. Potential is ideal and abstract, and not directly and immediately concerned with the constraints of the real world. Every business finds itself in such a situation. Business plans and targets can be set ideally but given the constraints of the real world, which include social, cultural, economic and political constraints, only some of them can be actualised. This implies that potential should always be understood against the background of constraints, those that dictate the actual state of affairs.

Now, one may understand these constraints in various ways. We could say that ethical concerns are not a constraint or we could factor them in our business plan. What JRD is attempting to give voice to, to find a space for, is the set of constraints which we have to necessarily accept. That is, defining the potential in terms of a larger space of constraints is actually an ethical principle which is equivalent to renouncement of our potential for the sake of something else. For example, I could have been somebody else, but I am what I am because I make conscious sacrifices. Finding a balance with what we are without a constant demand that we reach an ideal potential is already an important restraint on the notion of unbridled material or monetary profit.

What does it mean to say that profit is the measure of the increase or enlargement of what is originally available? How do we understand the measure of increase? In other words, what is the implication of an increase in something? If we look at the world exclusively through economic categories, the meaning of increase is the increase in economic worth. For example, in monetary terms, consider a case where my initial deposit of Rs 100 has increased to Rs 200, thereby making a profit of Rs 100. The increase is obvious if measured in terms of monetary value. Now suppose that in making my profit I lost a great deal of my mental peace. The loss of this peace cannot be monetarily translated and so there is an ambiguity as to how much I have really profited in this transaction. The basic problem here is that increase is best measured if the initial and final costs belong to the same kind or family – which have a common unit such as money. The sameness of the initial and the final, so important for grasping the quantum of profit, actually poses a serious challenge to the very idea of profit. And it is this problem that JRD tried to understand and respond to throughout his life. One way to explore this issue further is by explicitly relating profit to both quantity and quality.

Qualitative profit and quantitative profit

We can profit in many different ways from our actions. Some of them generate wealth. Sometimes there may be no increase in wealth but an increase in satisfaction or joy. Often we do something because it gives us happiness. Each one of these changes is a growth and is a profit. We profit not only in material ways but also in various other intangible ways. For example, after I conduct a transaction I may not have made profit in monetary terms but I might have attained a sense of peace in doing that act. It is important to acknowledge that this act too is profitable. Unfortunately, profit has come to be seen largely in terms of quantitative measures. This is part of an emphasis on quantitative understanding of the world, an understanding which has come to influence our private lives. The quantitative understanding of our world is significantly influenced by the growth of modern science. A fundamental shift in a worldview, and one which catalysed the growth of modern science, was the belief that science should be described in quantitative terms. Mathematics − numbers as a basic constituent of it − therefore became central to science.

The power of quantitative expressions lies in their ability to be objectively understood. For example, to say that there is a profit of Rs 100 seems to capture the nature of profit in contrast to a statement that says that one profited in some way. However, there is too much emphasis on the quantification aspect of profit. Non-material profit, such as attaining a state of contentment through some action, is also equally important. The problem is the apparent lack of comparison between different measures of profit.

It is long known that there are many aspects of life that are qualitative in character. These are not countable or measurable nor expressible in numerical units. Taste is one such example. We normally say that something tastes good but it might be stretching it a bit to say that the taste is 100 units of some measure. Our experience too is qualitative in character. The challenge is to express this qualitativeness in terms of more common accessible language. For example, let us say an action of mine leads to greater happiness. Another action also leads to happiness. How can I compare these two states of happiness? How can I know which one is a 'better' or more 'efficient' way to reach happiness? If happiness is quantifiable then it is quite easy to answer the above questions because I can say that the first action was quantified by x units and the second by y units. But if there is no quantitative measure for happiness then how can I compare different states of happiness? In our personal experience, we do know which action causes 'more' happiness but the problem is in converting this personal awareness of the 'more' into an objective measure.

The problem is magnified when applied to the idea of growth. If something is growing then it is useful to know by how much it has grown, how to compare different rates of growth and so on. Qualitative measures cannot do this, at least not as efficiently as quantitative measures. Thus, profit understood in the model of growth is almost always described in terms of quantifiable parameters.

But having accepted this, we need to expand the vocabulary associated with profit since it cannot be restricted to quantifiable parameters. Profit can happen in many different ways and many of the modes of profiting cannot be expressed in terms of numbers or percentage of increase. Some of these have to do with the improvement in the quality of living not only of the employees of an organisation but also of the larger community around a business concern.

It is the acknowledgement of the importance of these qualitative expressions of profit that we find first in JRD. Much before any of his peers, he had initiated various welfare measures not only for his employees but also for the community based on the belief that the presence of his companies should be a 'profit' for all those residing nearby. For JRD, profit thus cannot be a dirty word and in fact is quite the opposite. Profiting means enhancing the quality of not only business practices but also of living. It means enhancing not just one's own quality of life but also the quality of life of as many people as we can, especially those who are underprivileged. In recent times, these qualitative aspects of profit and business are becoming part of global business ethos, as manifested in the new mantra of Corporate Social Responsibility (CSR). A mix of quantitative and qualitative seems to be needed to have a balanced view of profit and ways of attaining profit. As we saw in the earlier chapters, we could say that JRD, in many different ways, attempted to expand the vocabulary of profit and create a more comprehensive meaning of profit.

Profit and ownership

There is an important issue of ownership that is essentially connected with the idea of profit. It is worth noting this, especially since JRD's actions reflect his great sensitivity to the idea of ownership. How much of the incentive towards growth and profit comes from a notion of ownership and belongingness? Can there be profitable growth in organisations when there is no sense of ownership in those who contribute to the growth of the company?

There is a well-known link between ownership and profit, particularly individual ownership. The principle that an individual can 'own' an enterprise is one of the basic beliefs of a business community. Ownership of an enterprise, whether it be a small shop or a big factory, is often understood to be the motivation for making that enterprise profitable. Thus, the common wisdom about ownership, one that is reflected in various other ways even in more complex articulations of ownership in larger businesses, is that if one owns something then there is an incentive to make that profitable. Models where workers share in the ownership of an enterprise seem to have done comparably better than if they were merely employees.

However, owning a company has been understood not just as a catalysis for profit but as giving one the right to own the profits of the company. Private companies function on the belief that owning a company means owning its profits as well. At one level this is obviously true but at a deeper level there are various troubling issues.

JRD attempted to articulate the notion of *responsibility* towards profits. In this context, the following questions become important. Does an owner own the profits as well? Does she own all the profits? Or is it mandatory for the owner to stake a claim only to part of the profits?

Issues about ownership are as follows. Is there a deeper engagement with a concern if one owns at least a part of it? What is the implication of ownership here? Usually, ownership is understood not just as owning the company or part of it but owning an equivalent share of the profits. Thus, one of the most important meanings of ownership comes from its relationship to profit. In other words, if a stakeholder has no stake in the profit then how much of an involvement does the individual have in that company?

We have seen how government concerns, by and large, have been plagued by an indifferent approach to their governance since the people who ran these concerns did not relate themselves as owners of these concerns. In our country, we have also seen how public services are badly misused since people do not relate themselves as the 'owners' of these public utilities. Unfortunately, this has meant that people who do not feel an ownership with the organisations they belong to also become indifferent to it at the least and at the other extreme exploit it for their personal benefit.

There are two different ways of exhibiting the sense of ownership. One is feeling a sense of belonging to organisations that are not really one's own and work as if one would if the organisation belonged to oneself. And the other is to use the organisation for one's personal benefits thereby exhibiting a sense of ownership. The exploitation of government organisations by individuals reflects this extreme interpretation of ownership.

On the other hand, we have the example of JRD, who, as the Chairman of Air-India, set high standards of commitment and efficiency towards that government organisation. He exhibited a responsibility towards it as if it were one of the Tata companies.

Therefore, ownership can be understood in two ways: one is a sense of *responsibility* towards what we own and the other is the sense of *authority* over what we own. It may be argued that in the case of government or public institutions, one can only have a sense of responsibility and not authority in that one is only doing the job of safeguarding, protecting and enhancing the public institution to which one belongs. This view is one of trusteeship discussed earlier, wherein we accept that being the leader of a public institution is to be a trustee of it on behalf of others. As we discussed earlier, for Gandhi and JRD trusteeship was not only about responsibility towards public institutions but also something to be manifested in private institutions. So, in the case of public institutions, a sense of ownership can only be a sense of responsibility. No individual, however senior in the hierarchy of the institution, can claim authority over such institutions. Therefore, in such a case, the relationship between profit and ownership cannot be reduced merely to a difference in the input–output calculus. Since there is already a notion of responsibility inherent in owning the public company, there is also a factor of responsibility which will influence the definition of profit.

In the case of private companies, ownership is somewhat more complex. In the case of private property (including private businesses), the sense of responsibility is of course there. But there is also a sense of authority, one which is exemplified by the belief that what we own is indeed ours in a legal and moral sense. Authority over what is mine essentially implies that I have the freedom to do what I want with it. This also implies that I alone am responsible for the good or bad that comes out of my organisation. Thus, viewing ownership along the idea of authority changes the nature of owning and relating to all the others who belong to that institution. In such a scenario, profit may be shaped by more practical and material concerns.

Not all private companies can afford to take this view of ownership as authority. Those companies which have shareholders and financial institutions as partners have a responsibility towards them. In modern parlance, this view of responsibility is towards all stakeholders, which might include government, local community etc.

However, what JRD was aiming at was to understand ownership as responsibility even when one is an individual owner. *In other words, for JRD the distinguishing mark of ownership does not lie in how much authority we have over what we own but how much responsibility we have towards what we own.* The very idea of responsibility implies a responsibility that is much larger than the concerns of an individual. Thus, even before social audit became a buzzword for the private sector, JRD had already initiated that process in TISCO. The original vision of Jamsetji Tata essentially integrated a greater sense of responsibility that goes hand in hand with business. As described earlier, the Tatas from Jamsetji onwards have been instrumental in setting up many institutes and hospitals, which are now dedicated to the nation. In spite of their role in creating these institutions, the Tatas have no 'authority' over them although they have an incipient responsibility, which they at the most discharge through their representation in the official body of these institutions. Thus, they do not own them in the sense of authority. However, they own them, just as many others do, through their sense of responsibility that they share in the well-being of these institutions.

Thus, once profit and ownership are understood in terms of responsibility then there will immediately be a combination of quantitative and qualitative aspects of profit that will perforce be taken into account.

A related question is this: Once a company makes a profit, to whom does the profit belong? This question, at first sight, seems to have an obvious answer, namely, that it belongs to those who created the profit. However, this answer is not so simple as business concerns have long realised. Does the owner of a concern take all the profits or do people who are involved in the creation of the profit have a share in it? And if they do, how much of a share is reasonable? Further, how much of the profit should be ploughed back into the company to sustain future growth, modernisation and so on? These are not only difficult questions but also those which are dependent on particular situations. However, the broader issue is the question of putting profit back to use, not for personal gain but for the gain of the company, community and other stakeholders.

There is one notion of profit which is very closely aligned with this view of profit. This is the view that profit is necessary for expanding and for growing. Growth and profit are in a circular relation with one another. Profit allows expansion and expansion generates more profit. And if part of profit is set aside for public good then it is desirable to generate more profit. Therefore, we have a legitimate ethical reason for profiting; namely, profiting allows for greater service to the larger community.

The other responsibility of using profits in the right manner consists in sustaining the business at the level it is in, even if there is no further expansion. This is the responsibility which is owed to the workers and the community which is supported by a company's activities. So the owners (or their representatives) of companies have a responsibility towards sustaining the livelihood of the people who are dependent on them. Of course, as JRD always recognised, this also means that the workers also approach their work with a sense of responsibility.

Earlier, I mentioned that placing profit within a broader, more responsible worldview makes the means of profiting as important as the final measure of profit. This issue of the means has always been an important formulation in ethics and is basically the argument that while the goal is important, while success is necessary, the means by which we achieve them are also very important. The legal system and even folk narratives of justice are based on the simple observation that the end rarely justifies the means. The simplest, crude forms of moral injunctions too illustrate this in many different ways. In a more complex setting, as in business dealings which are associated with so many positive and negative factors, the identification of means is not only extraordinarily difficult but also elusive to grasp. For example, one common argument is that since a company generates employment of workers, who might otherwise not have any income or employment, the company has a right to frame any rules it wants. Although this was the situation in early industrialised complexes and in the private sector for a long time, it is now generally accepted that the workers should also have a say in the management of the company for better synergy and more efficient functioning of the company. If we bring in other aspects such as the local community, local resources, national resources and legality, we find that the means–end dichotomy, although capturing the spirit of an important ethical idea, might end up being impractical.

The problem is basically as follows. Other than obviously clear immoral or illegal means, every other way of dealing with a problem seems to be strongly context bound. Thus, although we might agree, as JRD did, that bribing is a wrong means to achieve a result or that violence towards workers is a wrong way to deal with conflict, such clear-cut 'wrong means' are few and far between. One of the reasons for this lack of clarity on what constitutes right and wrong methods for a given situation lies in the emphasis given to material profit as the driving force of business. If material or monetary profit is not the central concern of business and profit is seen to have both qualitative and quantitative aspects to it, then we can find ways to understand more tangibly the means that lead to an end.

Balancing the means and end is always going to be difficult. That is no excuse for not being conscious of the problems they pose to business organisations. It is also well known that ethical issues in business are also notoriously slippery. But all that can be done, all that JRD thought needed to be done, is to be conscious of the problems and to be faithful to some basic ethical and philosophical beliefs. If there is one lesson that can be learnt from JRD in this context it is that we cannot give up on an ethical problem just because it is difficult and complex but that we should always search for ways to *balance* various parameters in reaching a decision.

Ironically, in present times, JRD is the voice that we need to hear when we encounter thoughtless privatisation. This is ironic because throughout his life, JRD was a strong proponent for freedom to private sectors. He consistently spoke and wrote strongly against the attempts by the government to impose various kinds of controls over private enterprise. However, he was also the one who spoke in favour of a mixed economy, where the government's role in certain sectors was desirable. He also strongly believed in and acted upon the idea of corporate responsibility, primary of which was not to let profit be the driving concern at the expense of every other responsibility, including those to the community and nation. So, even as late as 1975, he did not demand that there be absolutely no controls. He accepted the inevitability of a mixed economy, if not wholeheartedly at least as an important catalyst for development. He wrote that the 'mixed economy be not merely tolerated but encouraged and treated as the main instrument of economic growth with social justice.'[3] I do not think JRD wanted this model of the mixed economy to stay forever but saw it as a necessary mode by which development, with the face of social justice, would take place. Thus, at the beginning of the new millennium, where private enterprise under the impact of globalisation is caught up in what seems to be an unregulated race, the words and actions of JRD must be a source of caution.

To explicate the more complex meanings of profit we need to analyse other fundamental themes that are related to it. It is no accident that some of the themes upon which JRD most reflected include the nature of the private and public, the relation between them, autonomy and accountability, and so on. These are also some of the themes that we need to consider to develop a more expanded meaning of profit and to clarify the very meaning of business itself. I have discussed these concepts in the earlier chapters so as to lead us to understand this complex meaning of profit discussed in this chapter. The next chapter will exemplify some of the points discussed here in terms of JRD's personal ethics. For JRD, the way one behaved in one's life is also the way one behaves in their business. The root of ethical thought is as much personal as it is social.

Notes

1 *Business Standard*, 2 September 1990.
2 Technically, in economics, we can describe this process in terms of markets, whether captive markets or created ones.
3 J. R. D. Tata. *Keynote*. Edited by S. A. Sabavala and R. M. Lala. Bombay: Tata Press Limited, 1986, p. 57.

7

BEING HUMAN

From personal to social ethics

We often tend to look at the lives of pioneers in terms of their work and forget that they were first and foremost human beings just like all of us. It is often said that we are not islands; this is true as much of our intellect as our cultural world. The intellect has to be understood alongside the other cohabiting elements such as the emotional and the physical. It is the body, mind and spirit that together fashion our idea of the individual. All three are essential windows through which we can get a glimpse into the nature of JRD's view of life. The first example of balance for JRD was the balance between the physical, emotional and the intellectual. It is in human interactions that we can see the strengths as well as the weaknesses of individuals; many of these traits are also seeds for their approach to their professional life.

JRD was not merely a successful industrialist or someone who was just a leader of an important business group. He also did not see himself as an intellectual. On the other hand, he always professed disappointment at his lack of formal, professional education. If his father had not died in 1926, JRD would have gone to Cambridge. He had great respect for the institution of education and this is well manifested in the significant support given to education and research by the Tata Trusts. Other than the many institutes they helped create, the Tata trusts have also supported various initiatives in primary education. Although not formally educated in the engineering profession, all accounts from the people in the Tata group and outside point to his sharp intellect, including his understanding of machines and processes. His love affair with machines began as a boy when he had a fascination with cars and this continued throughout his life, involving not only fast cars but also aeroplanes. The fact that he got the first pilot's licence in India is another well-known fact that needs no further elaboration.

The earlier chapters have already discussed various aspects of his intellectual world, especially his approach to the conduct of professional business, including the emphasis on some ethical aspects. Hopefully, this analysis gave an idea of the man behind the image. To complete this picture, we have to consider JRD's emotional responses, for it is in them that we can discern the human behind the thoughts. And perhaps we can also see how his outlook towards business was reflected in his outlook towards life in general. Given the overall theme of this book, I will restrict myself to certain aspects of his personality, particularly the influences on him and his personal ethics. If there is one lesson that can be usefully learnt in this context, it is that without personal ethics there can be no meaningful public or social ethics. JRD's personal ethics are not only seen in the way he conducted his business but also in the interactions with people he knew and those he didn't. They are also reflected in the enormous corpus of letters he wrote, both in a professional and personal capacity.

Finally, a few words about the spirit behind the man. For JRD, the spirit of living, living well and to the full, was, I believe, one of the most important aspects of his personality. The human spirit in all its manifestations was the canvas of life for JRD. And in all his interactions, we can see a constant theme influencing his actions, namely, the desire to embody best what it means to be a human being.

Being human

What does it mean to be human? To be human is to exhibit our human nature in our interactions with the world and society. Herein lies the problem, which is that it seems to be quite a tricky task to define what it is to be human. One influential approach has tried to define being human by identifying the essence of being human. Over the course of time, various characteristics have been seen as the essence of being human, such as human as rational, as a tool-maker, as a storyteller and so on. However, none capture the spirit of being human in all its complexity. But there is one common meaning that we ascribe to a behaviour which is seen as being human, namely, empathy. A command such as 'be human' or 'do not be inhuman' demands a particular kind of response, namely, to be caring, to show sympathy for other human beings, and so on.

Empathy is an important psychological response and this characteristic explains some aspects of JRD's personality. This does not mean that JRD was without human faults or that he was empathetic to all concerned. Such a glorified picture cannot be true. However, in his personal and public life, JRD consistently seemed to be expressing and translating feelings of empathy. JRD was emotionally distressed at the level of poverty in the country and the inability of people like him to eradicate at least its worst aspects. His voluntary action of introducing various measures for labour welfare was based on his empathy with the working class. The social welfare schemes discussed earlier and his belief in trusteeship all indicate the importance of empathy as an important psychological factor in his life. Empathy defines the nature of JRD's response to the world around him.

Our responses to the world have often been seen through the framework of two oppositions. They can be dominantly intellectual in that we analyse problems, think of effective solutions and methods for implementation of these solutions. The intellectual response to the world and the problems we face can be contrasted with the emotional response to them. I believe that for JRD the emotional response was as important as the intellectual response, especially in the area of social welfare. When he saw poverty or injustice he did not seem to respond to them only at an intellectual level. In a way, he *felt* the problem and that is the expression of empathy that informed his worldview. This is consistent with his response to the pleasures of living: experiencing and feeling were an integral part of his personality.

In what follows, I will consider a few aspects that were of some influence on his life. I begin with the role of tradition, one that he inherited from his father, a person who not only had an affectionate relationship with JRD but was also a strong influence on his professional life. What set JRD apart in his adult life was his unique individuality, one that seemed to relish the wide variety of experiences that life offered. Finally, I conclude with a discussion of how an ethical stance in one's personal life influences ethics in the social world. Since JRD's ethical practices are well known, I will only discuss his habit of writing and replying to letters as indicative of an ethical stance that is fundamentally humanistic.

The role of tradition

Tradition was extremely important to JRD. His father seemed to have had a profound influence on him. Right from an early age, JRD recognised that he had a tradition to live up to, as one who would follow in his father's footsteps and take care of their business. It is clear that JRD saw himself as taking on the mantle of business at an early age. Even at the age of fourteen, he wrote this letter to his father:

> I have been trying not to think of Papa, but now that you have mentioned it I can tell you that I have been regretting often, too often, to have left you at such a strained and difficult time and when there was so much experience and knowledge for me to get & help to give you.

As he grew older, his letters showed a spirit that somehow yearned to be free. JRD was partial to a good life even then but recognised his duty towards his father and the family business. JRD's early letters sometimes captured a sense of poignancy as he realised that he was having a good time in France while his father carried the burden of managing his business. As he grew older, it was quite obvious that he had begun to look forward to being back in India and getting involved in the family business. In 1921, he wrote to his father, 'How much I would like to begin at once to work in Bombay so as to be able to unburden in a few years of a part of your work.' In September 1921, as a seventeen-year-old, he again wrote:

> I hope more and especially, that you are always in good health and that your affairs progressing to your satisfaction don't weigh so heavily on you and that you have more rest than before. Oh! when shall I possibly help a bit and pull

to me a part of the burden. When? Why am I not older and in the business since some time already?

JRD went to England to learn English before he enrolled himself for a professional education. From Suffolk, in December 1921, he wrote to his father:

I hope that when I will enter the business, you won't be dissatisfied with me, that I will prove to have the stuff of a business man and that later you will be quite proud of me.

And in 1925, in another letter to his father, he referred to Gandhi's visit to Jamshedpur and was effusive in praise of his father. As the letter makes clear, he obviously realised the heritage that was due upon him and the strength he would need to carry it forward.

I have received however mail from the office, mainly the speeches made by Mahatma Gandhi and concerning his visit to our works. I see it was a very great success and was quite an event in India. I must say I was very glad to see your name mentioned so often and to see how responsible and important was your position. If a son can compliment his father I can say I was devilishly proud of you! And I feel rather awed when I think that one day I will have to take your place. It will be a terribly heavy and great 'heritage' and I pray to god that I may have the brains, the willpower and the shoulders to bear the weight of it.

JRD was very conscious of the heritage and tradition that he belonged to. Psychologists often like to trace childhood influences for adult patterns of behaviour. In the case of JRD, the expectation of him, both from his father and himself, was a catalyst that might have made him aware of the fundamental importance of the sense of duty. His father also played a conscious role in this by stressing this aspect in many of his letters.

At the same time, JRD was a boy of great spirit, who exhibited the confusion and brashness of the young. He wrote prolifically – to his father, mother, siblings – and his letters show a great affection for his father and his family in general. The other consistent trait in these letters was his sense of humour, many times self-deprecating. The latter stayed with him through his life.

Individuality

Like any adolescent teenager, JRD was quite conscious of his self-image and many of his jokes were directed towards this aspect. Although in later years he was reputed to have had a strong personality and great charm, in his younger days he seemed to have been quite concerned about his frail physique, bouts of sickness and his long nose! Many letters were about his frail health and his attempts to do exercises to strengthen himself. One of them goes as follows:

As I promised you when you left I am doing regularly exercises every day two or three times, and I have bought a sandow exercises with which I develop my chest and its muscles. I have already made good progress. But the hardest part of my body to improve in shape and colour is my face; for though I feel I am getting much stronger, though I eat like ten hungry soldiers at every meal though I sleep so much and often, that I have acquired a strong reputation of laziness, my face is still pretty thin though not half so pale. And unluckily it's the face that people generally see first.

Writing in 1925 to his father, JRD exhibits his characteristic humour directed at his nose and his constant references to women and his love life, references that continue into his adult years.

It is a pity that Lulu Taleyarkhan has got such a big nose. I will feel very comfortable when I will be next to her! I was in love with her too, when I was a kid! Oh! Lala! What would our children be if we married! It is really remarkable the number of girls I have been in love with when I was a kid. I believe that up to 16 or 17 I was in love with every pretty girl or women I saw! Since then I have cooled down a lot! I haven't been in love for years. What a success!

The humour in his letters was also practically realised in his proclivity for jokes, which sometimes got him into trouble. Once he had invited S. S. Bhatnagar, the well-known scientist, who was then the Director of the National Chemical Laboratories. As per tradition for important visitors, Bhatnagar was invited to lunch with the other Directors in Bombay House. The jokes during lunch must have irritated Bhatnagar because after going back he wrote a letter to JRD, saying, among other things, that the marble floors of the National Chemical Laboratory, which were apparently discussed at the luncheon, were 'less expensive than the plastic floors planned for the TISCO Metallurgical Laboratory in Jamshedpur.' He continued, 'In a Board room or a Luncheon room of one's own, one can prove that black is white and white black and I think you pretty well succeeded in that on the 22nd April.' Unfortunately, Bhatnagar took some of the comments as a personal attack for he went on to add that 'Ours is a country in which all good efforts must be criticised.' JRD wrote back apologising and explained that the Directors' lunch room was 'well known for the banter and mutual ragging.' He then concluded the letter by writing, 'If, as I hope, you will lunch with us again some day, all levity will be strictly taboo!'[1]

Another facet of his personality that was not only present throughout his life but was also influential in his outlook of life was his passion for adventure and sports. His letters from France about buying a car, the Bugatti, are like that of any spoilt child writing to his father, albeit tinged with humour! He managed to convince his father to buy him the fancy sports car and soon, in 1921, when he was in England he wrote to his father about buying a bike. His letter sounds like one from any besotted seventeen-year-old, except in this case JRD's love was for a bike. In this letter he wrote:

I know what I ask you is terrible, considering your ideas and Mama's on a motorcycle which to you both is simply an instrument of accidents and death... I won't speak any more about it now, dear Papa, but please don't make a hasty decision and remember that I am, perhaps stupidly but really tremendously eager and hopeful. And don't say 'Ask Mama', for she said, 'Ask Papa'! ... I will be dreaming and hoping until I get your answer, and I pray god I may not be deceived.

If JRD had not been a businessman, he would have been a racer, either of motorbikes, cars or aeroplanes. Or perhaps he would have been a bodybuilder given his passion for maintaining his body even after he had reached a respectable old age! His passion for sports and adventure made him an avid weightlifter and skier even in his old age. It was important for his self-image to indulge in these activities even so late in his life. Sports did not seem to have been much of a competitive activity for him. With his usual touch of wit, he once wrote to his father, 'I played this week in the tennis tournament in Open Singles and Handicap Singles. In order not to spoil my previous and brilliant record I managed to be beaten in both events.' His outlook towards sports and adventure did not seem to be the aggressive, win-win mentality so much a part of modern corporate and management personality building but more of a pleasure in the activity of engaging in these activities.

There is something important in JRD's approach to sports that will also help us understand his life. The greatest challenges to JRD came principally from finding his boundaries and limitations. His competition was not a competition against others but only with his own capabilities. Thus, competitive sports did not seem to have much interested him, not as much as those needing individual skills where he was pitted against himself or, at the most, nature. The Aga Khan race illustrates this characteristic well. JRD was one of the participants in the Aga Khan race for the first solo flight from India to England or England to India. JRD flew from India to England and the eventual winner, Aspy Engineer, flew from England to India. It so happened that they met in Alexandria where Engineer was stranded because of the lack of spare plugs. JRD offered him four of his spares, which in the final analysis helped Engineer beat JRD in the race.[2] JRD never regretted his benevolence and in fact was quite happy that Engineer won since it helped him get into the Indian Air Force. For JRD, the great pleasure was already present in the act of flying and participating in that race.

I do not think it is an exaggeration to claim that the spirit of challenge which drove him was not based on the singular goal of 'winning' over others or for that matter competing with others in order to win. I believe that this attitude towards challenges in sports also influenced his business practice. The reasons for this claim are easy to understand. Playing, participating in the best way we can is the true measure of sportsmanship, although one that has gone out of fashion these days. This approach to sports is also related to the ethics of stressing the means as much as the end; that is, the way we do something is as important as the end product. This view privileges individuality but does not *define* individuality in opposition to other individuals. The model of sports or at least of certain games where to win means somebody else must lose is a model that defines the nature of one individual in contrast to the defeated individuals. That is exactly what the forgotten nature of sportsmanship was against. The balance between being an individual and yet part of the world of other individuals is another balancing act for JRD. One way of creating such a balance is to do things for oneself without seeing everything as a competition with another individual where one of the two has to win or do better. This personal worldview of JRD's translated into a social ethics of conducting business in particular ways.

The importance of individuality is also exemplified in his solo flights. JRD was the pilot of the first postal service in India in 1932. In 1982, when there was an occasion to celebrate the golden jubilee of this event, JRD insisted on flying solo in a similar plane from Karachi to Bombay. For JRD, this act was not to prove anything to others. He had already proved enough. This act was for JRD alone; it was a reaffirmation of his existence, of his capacity to derive pleasure from the act of living. One of the reasons for that flight, he said in an extempore speech after his flight, was the hope that it 'would rekindle a spark of enthusiasm, a desire to do something for the country' as well drive one to be a pioneer however discouraging the situation may be. He concluded by saying that he hoped that 'despite all the difficulties, all the frustrations, there is a joy in having done something as well as you could and better than others thought you could.'[3] The emphasis here is on the autonomy of the individual who can only strive to do the best he or she can; the measure for that is not in beating somebody else at something but of knowing that you have done your best. It is not an accident that JRD mentioned in an interview published in June 1992 that his epitaph would best read, 'He did his best.'[4]

The spirit of being a pioneer was thus captured in this spirit of adventure. Once he wrote to a friend:

> I think you are quite right in deploring the lack of spirit of adventure and a zest for living dangerously amongst the youth of India today. They do not know what fun they miss! While love of speed or danger is not a particularly useful quality in a man, a spirit of adventure is and the one cannot go without the other. The yearning for safety and security is a pretty deadening thing and I fear that too many of our educated youngsters suffer from it for our national good.[5]

Now, nearly fifty years later, JRD would perhaps say the same thing; only the situation regarding our educated youngsters may have become worse!

Personal and social ethics

We cannot lead an ethical life if our ethical actions in our private and public lives are contradictory. In other words, there is no point in being ethical in public life while following unethical practices in personal life. Morality in the case of the private–public divide occurs in yet another way: not using the public resources, which are anyway available to the individual, for private benefit. There are many anecdotes that reflect the ethical issues that arise in inhabiting both private and public life. One popular example is that of government servants (including politicians and bureaucrats) who would refuse to use their office supplies for private use. An apocryphal story about Sir Visveshwariah (who incidentally was a Director of TISCO for many years) was about how he would use his official pen only for his official correspondence and when he had to write personal correspondence he would use his personal pen. There are many such instances, especially in the life stories of the leaders of the Indian Independence movement.

Perhaps as a reflection of the times he lived in, JRD too exemplified this awareness of the ethical dimensions of private–public morality. In what follows, I want to discuss some aspects of this larger ethical world that was the bedrock of JRD's actions. While there are many examples to illustrate his ethical approach, I want to choose one particular example, that of letter writing. Although one might think that letter writing and ethics have no relationship, I would like to argue that JRD's letter writing illustrates a particular ethical view, one that will allow us to understand JRD in a more complete manner.

JRD received and wrote thousands of letters. He received a large number of personal mail. People who were absolute strangers would write to him. Some of the letters requested him to help with a particular problem, some wanted advice on a variety of topics, some asked for jobs, while others asked for gifts! JRD wrote back to most of them. In doing so, he was exemplifying a particular ethical stance, one that makes us understand his humanistic approach to life and business.

Letter writing is an interesting act. The ethical stance of a person who receives such letters can be quite ambiguous. Should one reply to all these letters? Should one do what one can if there are requests in these letters? And how do we choose which of the letter writers need genuine help? And so on.

For a public figure, replying to letters is an ethical imperative. When a stranger, who in most cases is in a more unfortunate condition than the receiver of the letter, writes to a public figure, he or she is appealing to this person. Whether one can help the letter writer or not is not the issue here. What is important is to respond back to the letter writer, thereby acknowledging and validating the existence of that person in the eyes of the person to whom the letter is addressed. In most cases, as we know in our own lives, not replying to a letter causes much more psychological disturbance than a letter which says that nothing can be done. Thus, every letter demands a response, whether it is from a friend or a stranger, and this was well understood by JRD. In responding to the letters he received, JRD was affirming the common humanity that connected him and the writer. This was an element of the empathy that characterised JRD's relationship with the social world.

Even something as prosaic as replying to letters is an art. It is an art that combines communication and emotion, and for public figures like JRD, whose letters were always destined to be public documents, there was a sense of history and responsibility. JRD learnt this lesson when he was young. In 1925, in one of the letters to his father, JRD wrote:

> I have received your letter of the 28th January and I thank you very much for it. I must admit that its perusal did not wholly fill me with joy which is normal, as it consists partly of a scolding. I replied to it the very day I received it, and after, very wisely tore it up. One should never write without being perfectly cool and even minded, and after the composition of your wire and your letter I was probably not that!

There are thousands of JRD letters. Many of them are very brief. Some of them are longer and these are mainly to close friends or those that involve a discussion on some policies. For JRD, replying to a letter was part of being ethically human. He belonged to an era where the ethics of letter writing was an important facet of the leaders of the time. Once, when writing about Gandhi he noted that Gandhi 'was also, like Jawaharlal Nehru, the most considerate and courteous of men who would never leave a question or a letter, however unimportant, unanswered.'[6] The influence of the times and his own ethical humanism influenced JRD's approach to letter writing.

In 1979, a woman wrote a letter to JRD complaining about the noise of a generator that was used by Hotel President in Bombay. She described how this noise was disturbing her family. JRD replied to her immediately, noting that although he had no role in the daily management of the hotel he had nevertheless spoken to the hotel management and as a first step they had agreed to use the generator only in the daytime. He also mentioned that he had been reassured that means for insulating the noise from generators were also being provided. In December 1990, there was another similar letter from a resident near the Taj West End Hotel in Bangalore. In response, JRD took immediate action. The woman wrote back to JRD after the problem was swiftly resolved. She wrote:

> As per your directions, the Chief Engineer of the Taj Group had visited Bangalore and we were today informed by... that new Thermopack cooling towers have been ordered and will be installed within a month. These towers... will certainly solve the serious problems we were facing... Your considerate action has also prevented what would otherwise have been a certain uprooting of a family as it would have been impossible for us to continue to live here.

As expected of a prominent personality like JRD and also given his leadership of the Tata group, there were a large number of letters asking for his help to get a job in the group. Many of these letters were requests for jobs for themselves or for their children or relations. There were letters asking for his support to become a pilot. In most cases where there was no possibility of any support, there was always a polite reply from JRD saying so. In some cases, information on whom to contact was also supplied. For young entrepreneurs he would write about what they could do or whom to contact. One striking aspect of these responses was with respect to people approaching him for jobs for their children or themselves. In many cases these were well-known people, including bureaucrats who were retired and people from royal families. In most such cases, JRD would reply saying that he did not interfere in the selection of candidates and at the most he would offer to forward the bio-data to the appropriate person within the organisation. Even when he did forward such cases, he would let the appropriate officer know that he was not recommending the case in any sense but only forwarding it to be considered in due process. He did this consistently whether it was a well-known personality who wrote to him or if it was a stranger.

However, in some cases he made an extra effort. A few of them were for people he was close to perhaps and more interestingly the other cases were for those who he thought deserved help. One example is an interesting illustration of this empathy. This was a letter from a young man in Allahabad in 1982. It began by saying that 'this letter goes out from one human being to another, strictly on personal basis, addressed to one who has made all success in life, from one who is about to begin life in its true perspective.' The writer added that his father was not keeping good health and therefore he had decided to take care of the family. He then asked JRD whether he could find a position under him. All he wanted, the young man wrote, was a 'fair chance'. JRD found something appealing in this letter. Not the request for the job but the way in which this person had phrased it. So he passed it on to various people in the organisation with the remark that if there were any tests and interviews for any job openings, they could call this person if found suitable. There was no intervention on his part and he just hoped that the due process might find this person capable of a job in one of their companies. He kept track of this case and in the jottings on the copy of his reply there is one which notes that this person was finally selected for a job in one of their concerns. What JRD was responding to was the sense of human spirit in the young man.

There were also cases of other young entrepreneurs writing for advice or blessing before starting their enterprise. In these cases, JRD always seemed to have made a point of replying back with some useful information. There were also many other kinds of letters. One such letter is an interesting example. A man from Germany wrote to JRD saying that he was born in India but lived in Germany. He then went on to say that he was interested in bringing solar technology to India. Not only was the letter written with quite a few mistakes but it also ended in this manner: 'If you are at all interested for a nearest talk I am glad to come down to you and accordingly please arrange for the return flight and accomodation (sic) at your cost.'

Perhaps not so surprisingly, quite a few letters like this were received by JRD. Like this one from an employee in Bangalore in 1981. It began by praising JRD, noting that the government had 'recognised in you the hidden treasure of knowledge and Wisdom', and further showered on him phrases such as 'brilliant Chairman', 'an industrialist of International Fame and Matchless Reputation' and so on. The letter then ended with: 'I shall be highly obliged, if you can kindly send me an Executive Bag, a Diary and Gift Articles of our Company for my personal use.'

Any public figure, especially those who are heads of a group of companies in which employment is sought after, probably received the kinds of letter JRD did. And perhaps some of the other stalwarts replied in a manner similar to JRD. However, the point that should interest us is the insight into JRD that is available through his massive correspondence. Insight not into his business acumen or management skills or even his political views (notwithstanding his caustic comments about the communists in some of these letters!) but into the nature of his being, of his outlook towards humanity, both in business and towards ordinary people.

It was this human touch that functions as a great metaphor in JRD's view of life, including his business relations. In this context, it is worth quoting from a letter of a retired TISCO employee who wrote to JRD after his retirement about the wonderful experience he had as an employee of the Tatas. In this letter he also recounted an incident. This person wrote:

> Smoking was a taboo in the General Office then, as now. I, however, had succeeded in making friends with... (dreaded by everyone else) and used to resort to the cosy comfort of her office for a quiet smoke. One day you surprised us by a sudden visit and as I was about to throw away the cigarette, you held my hand and said 'boy, that cigarette is expensive, don't throw it away'.

Anecdotes are perhaps like statistics: they hide more than they reveal. The personality of JRD cannot be constructed out of the thousands of anecdotes about him. They do show us glimpses of the man but to know the person behind these anecdotes we have to probe further into his motivations, beliefs and desires. There is much in the life of JRD that supplies material for analysing his intellectual positions and I have tried to do this in a limited manner in the previous chapters. There is also a foundation of his emotional, private life that can be discerned and inferred in his actions. However, this is a life that is visible only through the filter of the public eye and his public relations. For those who knew him, they had a great warmth for him. And perhaps this is not surprising. For although he was a man who no doubt had some shortcomings, perhaps like his temper, he was also one who strove consciously to respond to people's needs. He strove to find a personal ethics which he could apply consistently not just in his personal life but also in his public one. And in doing this, he had his own Golden Rule of ethics. JRD articulated his version of this rule in a reply to a letter written by a lady who was having some trouble with the flat she was living in, a flat in Bombay on land owned by the Indian Institute of Science. She wrote saying that she had some problem with one of their officers. JRD wrote back saying that he hoped that the person had got back to her to explain the matter. And he concluded by noting that, 'It is an unfortunate aspect of human nature that most people do not think of other people's feelings and sentiments as they would expect them to think about their own.'

We do not need complex ethical theories to understand JRD. Insights into his life, into his essence as a human being, are to be found hidden in the letters that he wrote to strangers, in the policies that changed the life of a tribal in Bihar, in the speeches he made to government, in the challenge he posed to private businesses, and most of all in the sacrifices he made in order to live a life the way he thought it ought to be lived.

Notes

1 Letter to Bhatnagar, May 1953.
2 R. M. Lala. *Beyond the Last Blue Mountain*. New Delhi: Viking, 1992, p. 88.
3 J. R. D. Tata. *Keynote*. Edited by S. A. Sabavala and R. M. Lala. Bombay: Tata Press Limited, 1986, p. 33.
4 Interview with Manek Davar, June 1992.
5 Letter to Talyarkhan, 1957.
6 *Keynote*, op. cit. 'Foreword', pp. xii–xiii.

8

CONCLUSION

It is important to understand JRD not only because he was the leader of an important business group but also because of the challenges he posed to uncritical living. But the real question is this: how do we engage with him now? How do we engage in dialogue with his ideas so that they are accepted or modified or even rejected after sufficient introspection? In the present age of globalisation and liberalisation, are JRD's ideas relevant at all? More importantly, are his ideas relevant even within the larger Tata organisations?

JRD's philosophy would challenge any business, including his own, in present times. There are new challenges facing all businesses in the current era. We have seen the mushrooming of the service sector. The IT boom is transforming the ethos and practice of business as well as the broader culture. Traditional ideas of labour, including working hours and the nature of jobs, have undergone qualitative changes. One positive aspect of globalisation has been the insistence on various mechanisms that will ensure not only consistent quality but also certain ethical practices, including financial and environmental practices. However, since the nature of labour itself is undergoing change, new challenges arise, especially regarding taking an ethical stand on some of these issues.

Since the Tata companies have to respond to the challenges posed by other similar companies, the importance given to abstract principles becomes diluted. For example, a company such as Tata Consultancy Services (TCS) has to respond primarily to the culture of IT companies all over the world. This includes specific modes of management, salary structure and a different construction of the idea of labour. This is also one industry where changes are extremely rapid and sensitive to influence from across the world. Culturally, even the very notion of time is constructed differently for this sector. In such a case, how would companies within this industry engage with JRD in a meaningful manner? But, at the same time, I would argue that it is precisely these kinds of business that should take JRD seriously!

Changing times demand changes in our attitudes and responses. For example, in the early part of the last century and after Independence, there was a demand for certain industries necessary for the country. Jamsetji and JRD believed that they should establish such industries as they would be beneficial to the country. What does one do now in the twenty-first century? The idea of the nation itself has undergone change. The social forces that influence the policies of the government are different. The broader ethical climate of the country is much more turbulent than in previous times. Thus, the great challenge to the Tata group of companies lies in understanding the essential spirit embodied by the earlier leaders.

JRD spoke not just for the Tatas or only on behalf of them. His expectation of business standards was addressed to all other business as well. His suggestion of trusteeship was one that was applicable to the citizens of the country. Even within the Tatas, I do not believe that his views continue to have sustenance. This was a point that was also made in the social audit report of TISCO. This does not mean that JRD's views are primarily meant for those belonging to the Tatas. JRD is too important to be left only to the Tatas, and the challenge to engage with him, especially regarding his notions of responsibility and trusteeship, is one that all of us have to face.

As an example, consider the functioning of the many Trusts that are part of the Tata group. There are sources of conflict and confusion in the vision of these Trusts. What kind of work should they support? What is their ethical responsibility as philanthropists? Who are the stakeholders in making these decisions? I do not think the Trusts have been able to incorporate these questions into their daily functioning. Like some other Trusts, financial probity seems to have become the end-all of philanthropy. Lacking a framework by which to respond to the different ethical challenges of philanthropy discussed in this book, the Tatas are tending to become like other philanthropic organisations. This lack of accountability of the funders has also had a serious impact on many of the philanthropic initiatives. The case of the last institute founded by JRD, the National Institute of Advanced Studies (NIAS), Bangalore, is a case in point. There is little of the original vision of JRD in the institute now. Moreover, the Tatas by first being hands-off and then later intervening without expert knowledge, have caused the institute to become a classic example of how not to run institutions. More than mere administrative issues, there are troubling ethical problems in this case. What could have been one of the major success stories in humanities and social science initiatives in India has been completely compromised by the attitudes described earlier in the chapter on ethics. One was the lack of domain knowledge of the fields of study at NIAS, another was the inherent suspicion mentioned earlier but in this case transferred to a suspicion of the relevance and importance of the fields of social sciences and humanities, the third was a technocratic and managerial view of running a research institute and fourth was the corporate and scientific mentality of a suspicion towards issues of social justice and the ethics of representation. Even though this institute has had a very high attrition rate (especially compared to academic institutions in general), the Tatas, as prominent funders, have not insisted on any ethical codes of conduct of the leadership in the institute other than those related to accounting and finance. They have not shown any inclination to force the institute to be more democratic and egalitarian, and have thereby compromised on the quality of work produced there. A basic ethical response to complaints and whistleblowers has not been forthcoming. While representatives of private groups have often complained about the lack of support for merit in government institutions, the private groups in India have done the same by promoting and rewarding sycophancy and loyalty at the expense of academic integrity, as in the case of NIAS. The lack of response to complaints of ethical misconduct is a classic sign of the belief that the funders cannot be held to any standard of accountability. But such actions have also led to a serious social impact on the academic community in India and therefore there must be a greater sense of accountability that should be demanded of the institution as well as the funders.

However, having said this, I must also note that JRD's lack of theorising also leads to some confusion. Since he did not discuss his ideas, for example on ethics, in a theoretical framework it becomes difficult to know how to extend them to contexts different from those he encountered. It is in this respect that larger theoretical frameworks are necessary since ideally they would be independent of specific contexts and therefore allow applicability across a wider range of contexts and situations. What I have tried to do in this book is to expand the theoretical space around some of the themes that were important to JRD. More sustained extension and exploration is needed before we can place JRD's ideas within a coherent theoretical framework.

JRD was also a product of his times and was surrounded by other great personalities who set high standards in their private and public lives. He was influenced by Gandhi, had an affectionate regard for Nehru, felt inspired by Sardar Patel and was close to Jayaprakash Narayan. Thus, the inspiration of the times gave him the strength to lead his life the way he did. If we look at our leaders today, what inspiration can one draw from them?

The problem about becoming a great personality is that there is a tendency to make token gestures towards their thought. The case of Gandhi illustrates this very well. Gandhian organisations face great challenges to their very existence. Practice of Gandhian ideals, even among Gandhians, is becoming a rarity. In these changing times, there are many challenges to their basic principles. Negotiating with these challenges demands great intellectual and practical involvement, which many of them are not in a position to practice.

I do not believe that JRD will go the way of Gandhi as far as his organisation is concerned. His 'heirs' belong to a dynamic group that can, if they so desire, maintain his vision and expectations. They are an integral part of the mainstream society and thus their survival is much easier than the Gandhian organisations. And most importantly, the institutionalisation of some of JRD's ideals will ensure their continuity.

It is not the case that all the problems faced by JRD and his team were handled perfectly. Some of them were and some were not. There was also ambiguity about some important issues. But these were also the consequences of not accepting a situation but trying to overcome it. They arose in the very nature of trying – trying to find a balance, trying to follow ethical principles, trying to be human, and so on. One important characteristic of this constant trying was the capacity to take bold decisions against the grain of common practice, including decisions about labour and social responsibility when they were unfashionable. More than his business acumen and leadership, part of which lay in his choosing excellent people who had control over the companies they managed, it is this broader vision of excellence and leadership, coupled intrinsically with ethics, which is of great relevance today.

INDEX

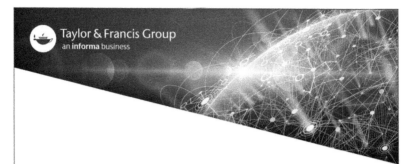

For Product Safety Concerns and Information please contact our EU
representative GPSR@taylorandfrancis.com
Taylor & Francis Verlag GmbH, Kaufingerstraße 24, 80331 München, Germany

www.ingramcontent.com/pod-product-compliance
Ingram Content Group UK Ltd.
Pitfield, Milton Keynes, MK11 3LW, UK
UKHW020946180425
457613UK00019B/539

* 9 7 8 0 3 6 7 4 8 7 1 2 6 *